FOREWORD

The collection of "Everything Will Be Okay" travel phrasebooks published by T&P Books is designed for people traveling abroad for tourism and business. The phrasebooks contain what matters most - the essentials for basic communication. This is an indispensable set of phrases to "survive" while abroad.

This phrasebook will help you in most cases where you need to ask something, get directions, find out how much something costs, etc. It can also resolve difficult communication situations where gestures just won't help.

This book contains a lot of phrases that have been grouped according to the most relevant topics. A separate section of the book also provides a small dictionary with more than 1,500 important and useful words.

Take "Everything Will Be Okay" phrasebook with you on the road and you'll have an irreplaceable traveling companion who will help you find your way out of any situation and teach you to not fear speaking with foreigners.

TABLE OF CONTENTS

T&P Books Publishing

T&P Books Publishing

PHRASEBOOK

— FRENCH —

THE MOST IMPORTANT PHRASES

This phrasebook contains
the most important
phrases and questions
for basic communication
Everything you need
to survive overseas

By Andrey Taranov

T&P BOOKS

Phrasebook + 1500-word dictionary

English-French phrasebook & concise dictionary

By Andrey Taranov

The collection of "Everything Will Be Okay" travel phrasebooks published by T&P Books is designed for people traveling abroad for tourism and business. The phrasebooks contain what matters most - the essentials for basic communication. This is an indispensable set of phrases to "survive" while abroad.

Another section of the book also provides a small dictionary with more than 1,500 useful words arranged alphabetically. The dictionary includes a lot of gastronomic terms and will be helpful when ordering food at a restaurant or buying groceries at the store.

T&P Books Publishing
www.tpbooks.com

ISBN: 978-1-78492-448-5

This book is also available in E-book formats.
Please visit www.tpbooks.com or the major online bookstores.

PRONUNCIATION

Letter	French example	T&P phonetic alphabet	English example

Vowels

Letter	French example	T&P phonetic alphabet	English example
A a	cravate	[a]	shorter than in ask
E e	mer	[ɛ]	man, bad
I i [1]	hier	[j]	yes, New York
I i [2]	musique	[i]	shorter than in feet
O o	porte	[o], [ɔ]	drop, baught
U u	rue	[y]	fuel, tuna
Y y [3]	yacht	[j]	yes, New York
Y y [4]	type	[i]	shorter than in feet

Consonants

Letter	French example	T&P phonetic alphabet	English example
B b	robe	[b]	baby, book
C c [5]	place	[s]	city, boss
C c [6]	canard	[k]	clock, kiss
Ç ç	leçon	[s]	city, boss
D d	disque	[d]	day, doctor
F f	femme	[f]	face, food
G g [7]	page	[ʒ]	forge, pleasure
G g [8]	gare	[g]	game, gold
H h	héros	[h]	silent [h]
J j	jour	[ʒ]	forge, pleasure
K k	kilo	[k]	clock, kiss
L l	aller	[l]	lace, people
M m	maison	[m]	magic, milk
N n	nom	[n]	name, normal
P p	papier	[p]	pencil, private
Q q	cinq	[k]	clock, kiss
R r	mars	[r]	rolled [r]
S s [9]	raison	[z]	zebra, please
S s [10]	sac	[s]	city, boss
T t	table	[t]	tourist, trip
V v	verre	[v]	very, river
W w	Taïwan	[w]	vase, winter

Letter	French example	T&P phonetic alphabet	English example
X x [11]	expliquer	[ks]	box, taxi
X x [12]	exact	[gz]	exam, exact
X x [13]	dix	[s]	city, boss
X x [14]	dixième	[z]	zebra, please
Z z	zéro	[z]	zebra, please

Combinations of letters

ai	faire	[ɛ]	man, bad
au	faute	[o], [o:]	floor, doctor
ay	payer	[eɪ]	age, today
ei	treize	[ɛ]	man, bad
eau	eau	[o], [o:]	floor, doctor
eu	beurre	[ø]	eternal, church
œ	œil	[ø]	eternal, church
œu	cœur	[ø:]	first, thirsty
ou	nous	[u]	book
oi	noir	[wa]	watt, white
oy	voyage	[wa]	watt, white
qu	quartier	[k]	clock, kiss

ch	chat	[ʃ]	machine, shark
th	thé	[t]	tourist, trip
ph	photo	[f]	face, food
gu [15]	guerre	[g]	game, gold
ge [16]	géographie	[ʒ]	forge, pleasure
gn	ligne	[ɲ]	canyon, new
on, om	maison, nom	[ɔ̃]	strong

Comments

[1] before vowels
[2] elsewhere
[3] before vowels
[4] elsewhere
[5] before e, i, y
[6] elsewhere
[7] before e, i, y
[8] elsewhere
[9] between two vowels

[10] elsewhere
[11] most of cases
[12] rarely
[13] in dix, six, soixante
[14] in dixième, sixième
[15] before e, i, u
[16] before a, o, y

LIST OF ABBREVIATIONS

English abbreviations

ab.	-	about
adj	-	adjective
adv	-	adverb
anim.	-	animate
as adj	-	attributive noun used as adjective
e.g.	-	for example
etc.	-	et cetera
fam.	-	familiar
fem.	-	feminine
form.	-	formal
inanim.	-	inanimate
masc.	-	masculine
math	-	mathematics
mil.	-	military
n	-	noun
pl	-	plural
pron.	-	pronoun
sb	-	somebody
sing.	-	singular
sth	-	something
v aux	-	auxiliary verb
vi	-	intransitive verb
vi, vt	-	intransitive, transitive verb
vt	-	transitive verb

French abbreviations

adj	-	adjective
adv	-	adverb
conj	-	conjunction
etc.	-	et cetera
f	-	feminine noun
f pl	-	feminine plural
m	-	masculine noun
m pl	-	masculine plural
m, f	-	masculine, feminine

pl	-	plural
prep	-	preposition
pron	-	pronoun
v aux	-	auxiliary verb
v imp	-	impersonnel verb
vi	-	intransitive verb
vi, vt	-	intransitive, transitive verb
vp	-	pronominal verb
vt	-	transitive verb

T&P BOOKS

FRENCH PHRASEBOOK

This section contains
important phrases that may
come in handy in various
real-life situations.
The phrasebook will help
you ask for directions, clarify
a price, buy tickets, and
order food at a restaurant

T&P Books Publishing

PHRASEBOOK CONTENTS

T&P Books Publishing

The bare minimum

Excuse me, ...	**Excusez-moi, ...** [ɛkskyze mwa, ...]
Hello.	**Bonjour** [bɔ̃ʒuːr]
Thank you.	**Merci** [mɛrsi]
Good bye.	**Au revoir** [o rəvwaːr]
Yes.	**Oui** [wi]
No.	**Non** [nɔ̃]
I don't know.	**Je ne sais pas.** [ʒə nə sɛ pɑ]
Where? | Where to? | When?	**Où? | Où? | Quand?** [u? | u? | kɑ̃?]

I need ...	**J'ai besoin de ...** [ʒe bəzwɛ̃ də ...]
I want ...	**Je veux ...** [ʒə vø ...]
Do you have ...?	**Avez-vous ... ?** [ave vu ...?]
Is there a ... here?	**Est-ce qu'il y a ... ici?** [ɛs kilja ... isi?]
May I ...?	**Puis-je ... ?** [pɥiʒ ...?]
..., please (polite request)	**..., s'il vous plaît** [..., sil vu plɛ]

I'm looking for ...	**Je cherche ...** [ʒə ʃɛrʃ ...]
restroom	**les toilettes** [le twalɛt]
ATM	**un distributeur** [œ̃ distribytœːr]
pharmacy (drugstore)	**une pharmacie** [yn farmasi]
hospital	**l'hôpital** [lɔpital]
police station	**le commissariat de police** [lə kɔmisarja də polis]
subway	**une station de métro** [yn stasjɔ̃ də metro]

taxi	**un taxi** [œ̃ taksi]
train station	**la gare** [la gar]

My name is ...	**Je m'appelle ...** [ʒə mapɛl ...]
What's your name?	**Comment vous appelez-vous?** [kɔmɑ̃ vuzaple-vu?]
Could you please help me?	**Aidez-moi, s'il vous plaît.** [ɛde-mwa, sil vu plɛ]
I've got a problem.	**J'ai un problème.** [ʒe œ̃ prɔblɛm]
I don't feel well.	**Je ne me sens pas bien.** [ʒə nə mə sɑ̃ pɑ bjɛ̃]
Call an ambulance!	**Appelez une ambulance!** [aple yn ɑ̃bylɑ̃:s!]
May I make a call?	**Puis-je faire un appel?** [pɥiʒ fɛr œn apɛl?]

I'm sorry.	**Excusez-moi.** [ɛkskyze mwa]
You're welcome.	**Je vous en prie.** [ʒə vuzɑ̃pri]

I, me	**je, moi** [ʒə, mwa]
you (inform.)	**tu, toi** [ty, twa]
he	**il** [il]
she	**elle** [ɛl]
they (masc.)	**ils** [il]
they (fem.)	**elles** [ɛl]
we	**nous** [nu]
you (pl)	**vous** [vu]
you (sg, form.)	**Vous** [vu]

ENTRANCE	**ENTRÉE** [ɑ̃tre]
EXIT	**SORTIE** [sɔrti]
OUT OF ORDER	**HORS SERVICE | EN PANNE** [ɔr sɛrvis | ɑ̃ pan]
CLOSED	**FERMÉ** [fɛrme]

OPEN

OUVERT
[uvɛr]

FOR WOMEN

POUR LES FEMMES
[pur le fam]

FOR MEN

POUR LES HOMMES
[pur le zɔm]

Questions

Where?	**Où?** [u?]
Where to?	**Où?** [u?]
Where from?	**D'où?** [du?]
Why?	**Pourquoi?** [purkwa?]
For what reason?	**Pour quelle raison?** [pur kɛl rɛzɔ̃?]
When?	**Quand?** [kɑ̃?]

How long?	**Combien de temps?** [kɔ̃bjɛ̃ də tɑ̃?]
At what time?	**À quelle heure?** [a kɛl œ:r?]
How much?	**C'est combien?** [sɛ kɔ̃bjɛ̃?]
Do you have ...?	**Avez-vous ... ?** [ave vu ...?]
Where is ...?	**Où est ..., s'il vous plaît?** [u ɛ ..., sil vu plɛ?]

What time is it?	**Quelle heure est-il?** [kɛl œr ɛ-til?]
May I make a call?	**Puis-je faire un appel?** [pɥiʒ fɛr œn apɛl?]
Who's there?	**Qui est là?** [ki ɛ la?]
Can I smoke here?	**Puis-je fumer ici?** [pɥiʒ fyme isi?]
May I ...?	**Puis-je ...?** [pɥiʒ ...?]

Needs

I'd like …	**Je voudrais …** [ʒə vudrɛ …]
I don't want …	**Je ne veux pas …** [ʒə nə vø pɑ …]
I'm thirsty.	**J'ai soif.** [ʒe swaf]
I want to sleep.	**Je veux dormir.** [ʒə vø dɔrmiːr]

I want …	**Je veux …** [ʒə vø …]
to wash up	**me laver** [mə lave]
to brush my teeth	**brosser mes dents** [brɔse me dɑ̃]
to rest a while	**me reposer un instant** [mə rəpoze œn ɛ̃stɑ̃]
to change my clothes	**changer de vêtements** [ʃɑ̃ʒe də vɛtmɑ̃]

to go back to the hotel	**retourner à l'hôtel** [rəturne a lotɛl]
to buy …	**acheter …** [aʃte …]
to go to …	**aller à …** [ale a …]
to visit …	**visiter …** [vizite …]
to meet with …	**rencontrer …** [rɑ̃kɔ̃tre …]
to make a call	**faire un appel** [fɛr œn apɛl]

I'm tired.	**Je suis fatigué /fatiguée/** [ʒə sɥi fatige]
We are tired.	**Nous sommes fatigués /fatiguées/** [nu sɔm fatige]
I'm cold.	**J'ai froid.** [ʒe frwɑ]
I'm hot.	**J'ai chaud.** [ʒe ʃo]
I'm OK.	**Je suis bien.** [ʒə sɥi bjɛ̃]

I need to make a call.	**Il me faut faire un appel.** [il mə fo fɛr œn apɛl]
I need to go to the restroom.	**J'ai besoin d'aller aux toilettes.** [ʒe bəzwɛ̃ dale o twalɛt]
I have to go.	**Il faut que j'aille.** [il fo kə ʒaj]
I have to go now.	**Je dois partir maintenant.** [ʒə dwa partir mɛ̃tnɑ̃]

Asking for directions

Excuse me, ...	**Excusez-moi, ...** [ɛkskyze mwa, ...]
Where is ...?	**Où est ..., s'il vous plaît?** [u ɛ ..., sil vu plɛ?]
Which way is ...?	**Dans quelle direction est ... ?** [dɑ̃ kɛl dirɛksjɔ̃ ɛ ... ?]
Could you help me, please?	**Pouvez-vous m'aider, s'il vous plaît?** [puve vu mɛde, sil vu plɛ?]

I'm looking for ...	**Je cherche ...** [ʒə ʃɛrʃ ...]
I'm looking for the exit.	**La sortie, s'il vous plaît?** [la sɔrti, sil vu plɛ?]
I'm going to ...	**Je vais à ...** [ʒə ve a ...]
Am I going the right way to ...?	**C'est la bonne direction pour ...?** [sɛ la bɔn dirɛksjɔ̃ pur ...?]

Is it far?	**C'est loin?** [sɛ lwɛ̃?]
Can I get there on foot?	**Est-ce que je peux y aller à pied?** [ɛskə ʒə pø i ale a pje?]
Can you show me on the map?	**Pouvez-vous me le montrer sur la carte?** [puve vu mə le mɔ̃tre syr la kart?]
Show me where we are right now.	**Montrez-moi où sommes-nous, s'il vous plaît.** [mɔ̃tre-mwa u sɔm-nu, sil vu plɛ]

Here	**Ici** [isi]
There	**Là-bas** [labɑ]
This way	**Par ici** [par isi]

Turn right.	**Tournez à droite.** [turne a drwat]
Turn left.	**Tournez à gauche.** [turne a goʃ]

first (second, third) turn

**Prenez la première
(deuxième, troisième) rue.**
[prəne la prəmjɛr
(døzjɛm, trwazjɛm) ry]

to the right

à droite
[a drwat]

to the left

à gauche
[a goʃ]

Go straight.

Continuez tout droit.
[kɔ̃tinɥe tu drwa]

Signs

WELCOME!	**BIENVENUE!** [bjɛ̃vny!]
ENTRANCE	**ENTRÉE** [ɑ̃tre]
EXIT	**SORTIE** [sɔrti]

PUSH	**POUSSEZ** [puse]
PULL	**TIREZ** [tire]
OPEN	**OUVERT** [uvɛr]
CLOSED	**FERMÉ** [fɛrme]

FOR WOMEN	**POUR LES FEMMES** [pur le fam]
FOR MEN	**POUR LES HOMMES** [pur le zɔm]
MEN, GENTS	**MESSIEURS (M)** [məsjø]
WOMEN, LADIES	**FEMMES (F)** [fam]

DISCOUNTS	**RABAIS	SOLDES** [rabɛ	sɔld]
SALE	**PROMOTION** [prɔmɔsjɔ̃]
FREE	**GRATUIT** [gratɥi]
NEW!	**NOUVEAU!** [nuvo!]
ATTENTION!	**ATTENTION!** [atɑ̃sjɔ̃!]

NO VACANCIES	**COMPLET** [kɔ̃plɛ]
RESERVED	**RÉSERVÉ** [rezɛrve]
ADMINISTRATION	**ADMINISTRATION** [administrasjɔ̃]
STAFF ONLY	**PERSONNEL SEULEMENT** [pɛrsɔnɛl sœlmɑ̃]

BEWARE OF THE DOG!	**ATTENTION AU CHIEN!** [atɑ̃sjɔ̃ o ʃjɛ̃!]
NO SMOKING!	**NE PAS FUMER!** [nə pɑ fyme!]
DO NOT TOUCH!	**NE PAS TOUCHER!** [nə pɑ tuʃe!]
DANGEROUS	**DANGEREUX** [dɑ̃ʒrø]
DANGER	**DANGER** [dɑ̃ʒe]
HIGH VOLTAGE	**HAUTE TENSION** [ot tɑ̃sjɔ̃]
NO SWIMMING!	**BAIGNADE INTERDITE!** [bɛɲad ɛ̃tɛrdit!]

OUT OF ORDER	**HORS SERVICE | EN PANNE** [ɔr sɛrvis | ɑ̃ pan]
FLAMMABLE	**INFLAMMABLE** [ɛ̃flamabl]
FORBIDDEN	**INTERDIT** [ɛ̃tɛrdi]
NO TRESPASSING!	**ENTRÉE INTERDITE!** [ɑ̃tre ɛ̃tɛrdit!]
WET PAINT	**PEINTURE FRAÎCHE** [pɛ̃tyr frɛʃ]

CLOSED FOR RENOVATIONS	**FERMÉ POUR TRAVAUX** [fɛrme pur travɔ]
WORKS AHEAD	**TRAVAUX EN COURS** [travɔ ɑ̃ kur]
DETOUR	**DÉVIATION** [devjasjɔ̃]

Transportation. General phrases

plane	**avion** [avjɔ̃]
train	**train** [trɛ̃]
bus	**bus, autobus** [bys, otɔbys]
ferry	**ferry** [feri]
taxi	**taxi** [taksi]
car	**voiture** [vwatyr]

schedule	**horaire** [ɔrɛr]
Where can I see the schedule?	**Où puis-je voir l'horaire?** [u pɥiʒ vwar lɔrɛ:r?]
workdays (weekdays)	**jours ouvrables** [ʒur uvrabl]
weekends	**jours non ouvrables** [ʒur nɔn uvrabl]
holidays	**jours fériés** [ʒur ferje]

DEPARTURE	**DÉPART** [depar]
ARRIVAL	**ARRIVÉE** [arive]
DELAYED	**RETARDÉE** [rətarde]
CANCELED	**ANNULÉE** [anyle]

next (train, etc.)	**prochain** [prɔʃɛ̃]
first	**premier** [prəmje]
last	**dernier** [dɛrnje]

When is the next ...?	**À quelle heure est le prochain ...?** [a kɛl œr ɛ lə prɔʃɛ̃ ...?]
When is the first ...?	**À quelle heure est le premier ...?** [a kɛl œr ɛ lə prəmje ...?]

When is the last ...?

À quelle heure est le dernier ...?
[a kɛl œr ɛ lə dɛrnje ...?]

transfer (change of trains, etc.)

correspondance
[kɔrɛspõdãs]

to make a transfer

prendre la correspondance
[prãdr la kɔrɛspõdãs]

Do I need to make a transfer?

Dois-je prendre la correspondance?
[dwaʒ prãdr la kɔrɛspõdãs?]

Buying tickets

Where can I buy tickets?	**Où puis-je acheter des billets?** [u pɥiʒ aʃte de bijɛ?]
ticket	**billet** [bijɛ]
to buy a ticket	**acheter un billet** [aʃte œ̃ bijɛ]
ticket price	**le prix d'un billet** [lə pri dœ̃ bijɛ]

Where to?	**Pour aller où?** [pur ale u?]
To what station?	**Quelle destination?** [kɛl dɛstinasjɔ̃?]
I need ...	**Je voudrais ...** [ʒə vudrɛ ...]
one ticket	**un billet** [œ̃ bijɛ]
two tickets	**deux billets** [dø bijɛ]
three tickets	**trois billets** [trwɑ bijɛ]

one-way	**aller simple** [ale sɛ̃pl]
round-trip	**aller-retour** [ale-rətur]
first class	**première classe** [prəmjɛr klɑs]
second class	**classe économique** [klɑs ekɔnɔmik]

today	**aujourd'hui** [oʒurdɥi]
tomorrow	**demain** [dəmɛ̃]
the day after tomorrow	**après-demain** [aprɛdmɛ̃]
in the morning	**dans la matinée** [dɑ̃ la matine]
in the afternoon	**l'après-midi** [laprɛmidi]
in the evening	**dans la soirée** [dɑ̃ la sware]

aisle seat

siège côté couloir
[sjɛʒ kote kulwar]

window seat

siège côté fenêtre
[sjɛʒ kote fənɛtr]

How much?

C'est combien?
[sɛ kɔ̃bjɛ̃?]

Can I pay by credit card?

Puis-je payer avec la carte?
[pɥiʒ peje avɛk la kart?]

Bus

bus	**bus, autobus** [otɔbys]
intercity bus	**autocar** [otɔkar]
bus stop	**arrêt d'autobus** [arɛ dotɔbys]
Where's the nearest bus stop?	**Où est l'arrêt d'autobus le plus proche?** [u ɛ larɛ dotɔbys lə ply prɔʃ?]
number (bus ~, etc.)	**numéro** [nymero]
Which bus do I take to get to …?	**Quel bus dois-je prendre pour aller à …?** [kɛl bys dwaʒ prãdr pur ale a …?]
Does this bus go to …?	**Est-ce que ce bus va à …?** [ɛskə sə bys va a …?]
How frequent are the buses?	**L'autobus passe tous les combien?** [lotɔbys pas tu le kõbjɛ̃?]
every 15 minutes	**chaque quart d'heure** [ʃak kar dœr]
every half hour	**chaque demi-heure** [ʃak dəmiœr]
every hour	**chaque heure** [ʃak œr]
several times a day	**plusieurs fois par jour** [plyzjœr fwa par ʒur]
… times a day	**… fois par jour** [… fwa par ʒur]
schedule	**horaire** [ɔrɛr]
Where can I see the schedule?	**Où puis-je voir l'horaire?** [u pɥiʒ vwar lɔrɛ:r?]
When is the next bus?	**À quelle heure passe le prochain bus?** [a kɛl œr pas lə prɔʃɛ̃ bys?]
When is the first bus?	**À quelle heure passe le premier bus?** [a kɛl œr pas lə prəmje bys?]
When is the last bus?	**À quelle heure passe le dernier bus?** [a kɛl œr pas lə dɛrnje bys?]

stop	**arrêt** [arɛ]
next stop	**prochain arrêt** [prɔʃɛn arɛ]
last stop (terminus)	**terminus** [tɛrminys]
Stop here, please.	**Pouvez-vous arrêter ici, s'il vous plaît.** [puve vu arɛte isi, sil vu plɛ]
Excuse me, this is my stop.	**Excusez-moi, c'est mon arrêt.** [ɛkskyze mwa, sɛ mɔ̃n arɛ]

Train

train	**train** [trɛ̃]
suburban train	**train de banlieue** [trɛ̃ də bɑ̃ljø]
long-distance train	**train de grande ligne** [trɛ̃ də grɑ̃d liɲ]
train station	**la gare** [la gar]
Excuse me, where is the exit to the platform?	**Excusez-moi, où est la sortie vers les quais?** [ɛkskyze mwa, u ɛ la sɔrti vɛr le ke?]

Does this train go to ...?	**Est-ce que ce train va à ...?** [ɛskə sə trɛ̃ va a ...?]
next train	**le prochain train** [lə prɔʃɛ̃ trɛ̃]
When is the next train?	**À quelle heure est le prochain train?** [a kɛl œr ɛ lə prɔʃɛ̃ trɛ̃?]
Where can I see the schedule?	**Où puis-je voir l'horaire?** [u pɥiʒ vwar lɔrɛːr?]
From which platform?	**De quel quai?** [də kɛl ke?]
When does the train arrive in ...?	**À quelle heure arrive le train à ...?** [a kɛl œr ariv lə trɛ̃ a ...?]

Please help me.	**Pouvez-vous m'aider, s'il vous plaît?** [puve-vu mɛde, sil vu plɛ?]
I'm looking for my seat.	**Je cherche ma place.** [ʒə ʃɛrʃ ma plas]
We're looking for our seats.	**Nous cherchons nos places.** [nu ʃɛrʃɔ̃ no plas]
My seat is taken.	**Ma place est occupée.** [ma plas ɛtokype]
Our seats are taken.	**Nos places sont occupées.** [no plas sɔ̃ ɔkype]

I'm sorry but this is my seat.	**Excusez-moi, mais c'est ma place.** [ɛkskyze mwa, mɛ sɛ ma plas]
Is this seat taken?	**Est-ce que cette place est libre?** [ɛskə sɛt plas ɛ liːbr?]
May I sit here?	**Puis-je m'asseoir ici?** [pɥiʒ maswar isi?]

On the train. Dialogue (No ticket)

Ticket, please.

I don't have a ticket.

I lost my ticket.

I forgot my ticket at home.

Votre billet, s'il vous plaît.
[vɔtr bijɛ, sil vu plɛ]
Je n'ai pas de billet.
[ʒə ne pɑ də bijɛ]
J'ai perdu mon billet.
[ʒe pɛrdy mɔ̃ bijɛ]
J'ai oublié mon billet à la maison.
[ʒe ublije mɔ̃ bijɛ a la mɛzɔ̃]

You can buy a ticket from me.

You will also have to pay a fine.

Okay.

Where are you going?

I'm going to ...

Vous pouvez m'acheter un billet.
[vu puve maʃte œ̃ bijɛ]
Vous devrez aussi payer une amende.
[vu dəvre osi peje yn amɑ̃d]
D'accord.
[dakɔ:r]
Où allez-vous?
[u ale-vu?]
Je vais à ...
[ʒə ve a ...]

How much? I don't understand.

Write it down, please.

Okay. Can I pay with a credit card?

Yes, you can.

Combien? Je ne comprend pas.
[kɔ̃bjɛ̃? ʒə nə kɔ̃prɑ̃ pɑ]
Pouvez-vous l'écrire, s'il vous plaît.
[puve vu lekrir, sil vu plɛ]
D'accord. Puis-je payer avec la carte?
[dakɔ:r. pɥiʒ peje avɛk la kart?]
Oui, bien sûr.
[wi, bjɛ̃ sy:r]

Here's your receipt.

Sorry about the fine.

That's okay. It was my fault.

Enjoy your trip.

Voici votre reçu.
[vwasi vɔtr rəsy]
Désolé pour l'amende.
[dezɔle pur lamɑ̃:d]
Ça va. C'est de ma faute.
[sa va. sɛ də ma fot]
Bon voyage.
[bɔ̃ vwaja:ʒ]

Taxi

taxi	**taxi** [taksi]
taxi driver	**chauffeur de taxi** [ʃofœr də taksi]
to catch a taxi	**prendre un taxi** [prɑ̃dr œ̃ taksi]
taxi stand	**arrêt de taxi** [arɛ də taksi]
Where can I get a taxi?	**Où puis-je trouver un taxi?** [u pɥiʒ truve œ̃ taksi?]
to call a taxi	**appeler un taxi** [aple œ̃ taksi]
I need a taxi.	**Il me faut un taxi.** [il mə fo œ̃ taksi]
Right now.	**maintenant** [mɛ̃tnɑ̃]
What is your address (location)?	**Quelle est votre adresse?** [kɛl ɛ vɔtr adrɛs?]
My address is ...	**Mon adresse est ...** [mɔn adrɛs ɛ ...]
Your destination?	**Votre destination?** [vɔtr dɛstinasjɔ̃?]
Excuse me, ...	**Excusez-moi, ...** [ɛkskyze mwa, ...]
Are you available?	**Vous êtes libre ?** [vuzɛt libr?]
How much is it to get to ...?	**Combien ça coûte pour aller à ...?** [kɔ̃bjɛ̃ sa kut pur ale a ...?]
Do you know where it is?	**Vous savez où ça se trouve?** [vu save u sa sə tru:v?]
Airport, please.	**À l'aéroport, s'il vous plaît.** [a laerɔpɔ:r, sil vu plɛ]
Stop here, please.	**Arrêtez ici, s'il vous plaît.** [arɛte isi, sil vu plɛ]
It's not here.	**Ce n'est pas ici.** [sə nɛ pɑ isi]
This is the wrong address.	**C'est la mauvaise adresse.** [sɛ la movɛz adrɛs]
Turn left.	**tournez à gauche** [turne a goʃ]
Turn right.	**tournez à droite** [turne a drwat]

How much do I owe you?	**Combien je vous dois?** [kɔ̃bjɛ̃ ʒə vu dwa?]
I'd like a receipt, please.	**J'aimerais avoir un reçu,** **s'il vous plaît.** [ʒɛmrɛ avwar œ̃ rəsy, sil vu plɛ]
Keep the change.	**Gardez la monnaie.** [garde la mɔnɛ]
Would you please wait for me?	**Attendez-moi, s'il vous plaît ...** [atɑ̃de-mwa, sil vu plɛ ...]
five minutes	**cinq minutes** [sɛ̃k minyt]
ten minutes	**dix minutes** [di minyt]
fifteen minutes	**quinze minutes** [kɛ̃z minyt]
twenty minutes	**vingt minutes** [vɛ̃ minyt]
half an hour	**une demi-heure** [yn dəmiœr]

Hotel

Hello.	**Bonjour.** [bɔ̃ʒuːr]
My name is ...	**Je m'appelle ...** [ʒə mapɛl ...]
I have a reservation.	**J'ai réservé une chambre.** [ʒe rezɛrve yn ʃɑ̃ːbr]
I need ...	**Je voudrais ...** [ʒə vudrɛ ...]
a single room	**une chambre simple** [yn ʃɑ̃br sɛ̃pl]
a double room	**une chambre double** [yn ʃɑ̃br dubl]
How much is that?	**C'est combien?** [sɛ kɔ̃bjɛ̃?]
That's a bit expensive.	**C'est un peu cher.** [sɛtœ̃pø ʃɛːr]
Do you have any other options?	**Avez-vous autre chose?** [ave vu otr ʃoːz?]
I'll take it.	**Je vais la prendre.** [ʒə ve la prɑ̃dr]
I'll pay in cash.	**Je vais payer comptant.** [ʒə ve peje kɔ̃tɑ̃]
I've got a problem.	**J'ai un problème.** [ʒe œ̃ prɔblɛm]
My ... is broken.	**... est cassé /cassée/** [... ɛ kase]
My ... is out of order.	**... ne fonctionne pas.** [... nə fɔ̃ksjɔn pɑ]
TV	**la télé ...** [la tele ...]
air conditioning	**air conditionné ...** [ɛr kɔ̃disjɔne ...]
tap	**le robinet ...** [lə rɔbinɛ ...]
shower	**ma douche ...** [ma duʃ ...]
sink	**mon évier ...** [mon evje ...]
safe	**mon coffre-fort ...** [mɔ̃ kɔfr-fɔr ...]

door lock	**la serrure de porte ...**
	[la seryr də pɔrt ...]
electrical outlet	**la prise électrique ...**
	[la priz elɛktrik ...]
hairdryer	**mon sèche-cheveux ...**
	[mɔ̃ sɛʃ ʃəvø ...]

I don't have ...	**Je n'ai pas ...**
	[ʒə ne pɑ ...]
water	**d'eau**
	[do]
light	**de lumière**
	[də lymjɛr]
electricity	**d'électricité**
	[delɛktrisite]

Can you give me ...?	**Pouvez-vous me donner ...?**
	[puve vu mə dɔne ...?]
a towel	**une serviette**
	[yn sɛrvjɛt]
a blanket	**une couverture**
	[yn kuvɛrtyr]
slippers	**des pantoufles**
	[de pɑ̃tufl]
a robe	**une robe de chambre**
	[yn rɔb də ʃɑ̃br]
shampoo	**du shampooing**
	[dy ʃɑ̃pwɛ̃]
soap	**du savon**
	[dy savɔ̃]

I'd like to change rooms.	**Je voudrais changer ma chambre.**
	[ʒə vudrɛ ʃɑ̃ʒe ma ʃɑ̃:br]
I can't find my key.	**Je ne trouve pas ma clé.**
	[ʒə nə truv pɑ ma kle]
Could you open my room, please?	**Pourriez-vous ouvrir ma chambre, s'il vous plaît?**
	[purje-vu uvrir ma ʃɑ̃:br, sil vu plɛ?]
Who's there?	**Qui est là?**
	[ki ɛ la?]
Come in!	**Entrez!**
	[ɑ̃tre!]
Just a minute!	**Une minute!**
	[yn minyt!]

Not right now, please.	**Pas maintenant, s'il vous plaît.**
	[pɑ mɛ̃tnɑ̃, sil vu plɛ]
Come to my room, please.	**Pouvez-vous venir à ma chambre, s'il vous plaît.**
	[puve vu vənir a ma ʃɑ̃:br, sil vu plɛ]

I'd like to order food service.	**J'aimerais avoir le service d'étage.** [ʒɛmrɛ avwar lə sɛrvis deta:ʒ]
My room number is ...	**Mon numéro de chambre est le ...** [mɔ̃ nymero də ʃɑ̃br ɛ lə ...]

I'm leaving ...	**Je pars ...** [ʒə par ...]
We're leaving ...	**Nous partons ...** [nu partɔ̃ ...]
right now	**maintenant** [mɛ̃tnɑ̃]
this afternoon	**cet après-midi** [sɛt aprɛmidi]
tonight	**ce soir** [sə swar]
tomorrow	**demain** [dəmɛ̃]
tomorrow morning	**demain matin** [dəmɛ̃ matɛ̃]
tomorrow evening	**demain après-midi** [dəmɛ̃ aprɛmidi]
the day after tomorrow	**après-demain** [aprɛdmɛ̃]

I'd like to pay.	**Je voudrais régler mon compte.** [ʒə vudrɛ regle mɔ̃ kɔ̃:t]
Everything was wonderful.	**Tout était merveilleux.** [tutetɛ mɛrvɛjø]
Where can I get a taxi?	**Où puis-je trouver un taxi?** [u pɥiʒ truve œ̃ taksi?]
Would you call a taxi for me, please?	**Pourriez-vous m'appeler un taxi, s'il vous plaît?** [purje-vu maple œ̃ taksi, sil vu plɛ?]

Restaurant

Can I look at the menu, please?	**Puis-je voir le menu, s'il vous plaît?** [pɥiʒ vwar lə məny, sil vu plɛ?]
Table for one.	**Une table pour une personne.** [yn tabl pur yn pɛrsɔn]
There are two (three, four) of us.	**Nous sommes deux (trois, quatre).** [nu sɔm dø (trwɑ, katr)]

Smoking	**Fumeurs** [fymœr]
No smoking	**Non-fumeurs** [nɔ̃-fymœr]
Excuse me! (addressing a waiter)	**S'il vous plaît!** [sil vu plɛ!]
menu	**menu** [məny]
wine list	**carte des vins** [kart de vɛ̃]
The menu, please.	**Le menu, s'il vous plaît.** [lə məny, sil vu plɛ]

Are you ready to order?	**Êtes-vous prêts à commander?** [ɛt-vu prɛ a kɔmɑ̃de?]
What will you have?	**Qu'allez-vous prendre?** [kale-vu prɑ̃dr?]
I'll have ...	**Je vais prendre ...** [ʒə ve prɑ̃dr ...]

I'm a vegetarian.	**Je suis végétarien.** [ʒə sɥi veʒetarjɛ̃]
meat	**viande** [vjɑ̃d]
fish	**poisson** [pwasɔ̃]
vegetables	**légumes** [legym]
Do you have vegetarian dishes?	**Avez-vous des plats végétariens?** [ave vu de pla veʒetarjɛ̃?]
I don't eat pork.	**Je ne mange pas de porc.** [ʒə nə mɑ̃ʒ pa də pɔːr]
He /she/ doesn't eat meat.	**Il /elle/ ne mange pas de viande.** [il /ɛl/ nə mɑ̃ʒ pa də vjɑ̃:d]
I am allergic to ...	**Je suis allergique à ...** [ʒə sɥi alɛrʒik a ...]

Would you please bring me ...	**Pourriez-vous m'apporter ...,** **s'il vous plaît.** [purje-vu mapɔrte ... , sil vu plɛ]
salt | pepper | sugar	**le sel | le poivre | du sucre** [lə sɛl | lə pwavr | dy sykr]
coffee | tea | dessert	**un café | un thé | un dessert** [œ̃ kafe | œ̃ te | œ̃ desɛr]
water | sparkling | plain	**de l'eau | gazeuse | plate** [də lo | gɑzøz | plat]
a spoon | fork | knife	**une cuillère | une fourchette |** **un couteau** [yn kɥijɛr | yn furʃɛt | œ̃ kuto]
a plate | napkin	**une assiette | une serviette** [yn asjɛt | yn sɛrvjɛt]
Enjoy your meal!	**Bon appétit!** [bɔn apeti!]
One more, please.	**Un de plus, s'il vous plaît.** [œ̃ də plys, sil vu plɛ]
It was very delicious.	**C'était délicieux.** [setɛ delisjø]
check | change | tip	**l'addition | de la monnaie |** **le pourboire** [ladisjɔ̃ | də la mɔnɛ | lə purbwar]
Check, please. (Could I have the check, please?)	**L'addition, s'il vous plaît.** [ladisjɔ̃, sil vu plɛ]
Can I pay by credit card?	**Puis-je payer avec la carte?** [pɥiʒ peje avɛk la kart?]
I'm sorry, there's a mistake here.	**Excusez-moi, je crois qu'il y a une** **erreur ici.** [ɛkskyze mwa, ʒə krwa kilja yn ɛrœr isi]

Shopping

Can I help you?

Est-ce que je peux vous aider?
[ɛskə ʒə pø vuzɛde?]

Do you have ...?

Avez-vous ... ?
[ave vu ...?]

I'm looking for ...

Je cherche ...
[ʒə ʃɛrʃ ...]

I need ...

Il me faut ...
[Il mə fo ...]

I'm just looking.

Je regarde seulement, merci.
[ʒə rəgard sœlmã, mɛrsi]

We're just looking.

Nous regardons seulement, merci.
[nu rəgardõ sœlmã, mɛrsi]

I'll come back later.

Je reviendrai plus tard.
[ʒə rəvjɛ̃dre ply ta:r]

We'll come back later.

On reviendra plus tard.
[õ rəvjɛ̃dra ply ta:r]

discounts | sale

Rabais | Soldes
[rabɛ | sɔld]

Would you please show me ...

Montrez-moi, s'il vous plaît ...
[mõtre-mwa, sil vu plɛ ...]

Would you please give me ...

Donnez-moi, s'il vous plaît ...
[dɔne-mwa, sil vu plɛ ...]

Can I try it on?

Est-ce que je peux l'essayer?
[ɛskə ʒə pø lesɛje?]

Excuse me, where's the fitting room?

Excusez-moi, où est la cabine d'essayage?
[ɛkskyze mwa, u ɛ la kabin desɛja:ʒ?]

Which color would you like?

Quelle couleur aimeriez-vous?
[kɛl kulœr ɛmərje-vu?]

size | length

taille | longueur
[taj | lõgœr]

How does it fit?

Est-ce que la taille convient ?
[ɛskə la taj kõvjɛ̃?]

How much is it?

Combien ça coûte?
[kõbjɛ̃ sa kut?]

That's too expensive.

C'est trop cher.
[sɛ tro ʃɛ:r]

I'll take it.

Je vais le prendre.
[ʒə ve lə prãdr]

Excuse me, where do I pay?	**Excusez-moi, où est la caisse?** [εkskyze mwa, u ε la kεs?]
Will you pay in cash or credit card?	**Payerez-vous comptant ou par carte de crédit?** [pεjre-vu kɔ̃tɑ̃ u par kart də kredi?]
In cash | with credit card	**Comptant | par carte de crédit** [kɔ̃tɑ̃ | par kart də kredi]

Do you want the receipt?	**Voulez-vous un reçu?** [vule vu œ̃ rəsy?]
Yes, please.	**Oui, s'il vous plaît.** [wi, sil vu plε]
No, it's OK.	**Non, ce n'est pas nécessaire.** [nɔ̃, sə nε pɑ nesesε:r]
Thank you. Have a nice day!	**Merci. Bonne journée!** [mεrsi. bɔn ʒurne!]

In town

Excuse me, please.	**Excusez-moi, ...** [ɛkskyze mwa, ...]
I'm looking for ...	**Je cherche ...** [ʒə ʃɛrʃ ...]
the subway	**le métro** [lə metro]
my hotel	**mon hôtel** [mɔn otɛl]
the movie theater	**le cinéma** [lə sinema]
a taxi stand	**un arrêt de taxi** [œn arɛ də taksi]
an ATM	**un distributeur** [œ̃ distribytœ:r]
a foreign exchange office	**un bureau de change** [œ̃ byro də ʃɑ̃ʒ]
an internet café	**un café internet** [œ̃ kafe ɛ̃tɛrnɛt]
... street	**la rue ...** [la ry ...]
this place	**cette place-ci** [sɛt plas-si]
Do you know where ... is?	**Savez-vous où se trouve ...?** [save vu u sə truv ...?]
Which street is this?	**Quelle est cette rue?** [kɛl ɛ sɛt ry?]
Show me where we are right now.	**Montrez-moi où sommes-nous,** **s'il vous plaît.** [mɔ̃tre-mwa u sɔm-nu, sil vu plɛ]
Can I get there on foot?	**Est-ce que je peux y aller à pied?** [ɛskə ʒə pø i ale a pje?]
Do you have a map of the city?	**Avez-vous une carte de la ville?** [ave vu yn kart də la vil?]
How much is a ticket to get in?	**C'est combien pour un ticket?** [sɛ kɔ̃bjɛ̃ pur œ̃ tikɛ?]
Can I take pictures here?	**Est-ce que je peux faire des photos?** [ɛskə ʒə pø fɛr de foto?]
Are you open?	**Êtes-vous ouvert?** [ɛt-vu uvɛ:r?]

When do you open?	**À quelle heure ouvrez-vous?** [a kɛl œr uvre-vu?]
When do you close?	**À quelle heure fermez-vous?** [a kɛl œr fɛrme-vu?]

Money

money	**argent** [arʒɑ̃]
cash	**argent liquide** [arʒɑ̃ likid]
paper money	**des billets** [de bijɛ]
loose change	**petite monnaie** [pətit mɔnɛ]
check | change | tip	**l'addition | de la monnaie | le pourboire** [ladisjɔ̃ | də la mɔnɛ | lə purbwar]

credit card	**carte de crédit** [kart də kredi]
wallet	**portefeuille** [portəfœj]
to buy	**acheter** [aʃte]
to pay	**payer** [peje]
fine	**amende** [amɑ̃d]
free	**gratuit** [gratɥi]

Where can I buy ...?	**Où puis-je acheter ... ?** [u pɥiʒ aʃte ...?]
Is the bank open now?	**Est-ce que la banque est ouverte en ce moment?** [ɛskə la bɑ̃k ɛtuvɛrt ɑ̃ sə mɔmɑ̃?]
When does it open?	**À quelle heure ouvre-t-elle?** [a kɛl œr uvr-tɛl?]
When does it close?	**À quelle heure ferme-t-elle?** [a kɛl œr fɛrm-tɛl?]

How much?	**C'est combien?** [sɛ kɔ̃bjɛ̃?]
How much is this?	**Combien ça coûte?** [kɔ̃bjɛ̃ sa kut?]
That's too expensive.	**C'est trop cher.** [sɛ tro ʃɛ:r]

Excuse me, where do I pay?	**Excusez-moi, où est la caisse?** [εkskyze mwa, u ε la kεs?]
Check, please.	**L'addition, s'il vous plaît.** [ladisjɔ̃, sil vu plε]
Can I pay by credit card?	**Puis-je payer avec la carte?** [pɥiʒ peje avεk la kart?]
Is there an ATM here?	**Est-ce qu'il y a un distributeur ici?** [εskilja œ̃ distribytœ:r isi?]
I'm looking for an ATM.	**Je cherche un distributeur.** [ʒə ʃεrʃ œ̃ distribytœ:r]

I'm looking for a foreign exchange office.	**Je cherche un bureau de change.** [ʒə ʃεrʃ œ̃ byro də ʃɑ̃:ʒ]
I'd like to change ...	**Je voudrais changer ...** [ʒə vudrε ʃɑ̃ʒe ...]
What is the exchange rate?	**Quel est le taux de change?** [kεl ε lə to də ʃɑ̃:ʒ?]
Do you need my passport?	**Avez-vous besoin de mon passeport?** [ave vu bəzwɛ̃ də mɔ̃ paspɔ:r?]

Time

What time is it?	**Quelle heure est-il?** [kɛl œr ɛ-til?]
When?	**Quand?** [kɑ̃?]
At what time?	**À quelle heure?** [a kɛl œ:r?]
now | later | after ...	**maintenant | plus tard | après ...** [mɛ̃tnɑ̃ | ply tar | aprɛ ...]

one o'clock	**une heure** [yn œ:r]
one fifteen	**une heure et quart** [yn œ:r e kar]
one thirty	**une heure et demie** [yn œ:r e dəmi]
one forty-five	**deux heures moins quart** [døzœr mwɛ̃ kar]

one | two | three	**un | deux | trois** [œ̃ | dø | trwɑ]
four | five | six	**quatre | cinq | six** [katr | sɛ̃k | sis]
seven | eight | nine	**sept | huit | neuf** [sɛt | ɥit | nœf]
ten | eleven | twelve	**dix | onze | douze** [dis | ɔ̃z | duz]

in ...	**dans ...** [dɑ̃ ...]
five minutes	**cinq minutes** [sɛ̃k minyt]
ten minutes	**dix minutes** [di minyt]
fifteen minutes	**quinze minutes** [kɛ̃z minyt]
twenty minutes	**vingt minutes** [vɛ̃ minyt]

half an hour	**une demi-heure** [yn dəmiœr]
an hour	**une heure** [yn œ:r]

in the morning	**dans la matinée** [dɑ̃ la matine]
early in the morning	**tôt le matin** [to lə matɛ̃]
this morning	**ce matin** [sə matɛ̃]
tomorrow morning	**demain matin** [dəmɛ̃ matɛ̃]

at noon	**à midi** [a midi]
in the afternoon	**dans l'après-midi** [dɑ̃ laprɛmidi]
in the evening	**dans la soirée** [dɑ̃ la sware]
tonight	**ce soir** [sə swar]

at night	**la nuit** [la nɥi]
yesterday	**hier** [jɛr]
today	**aujourd'hui** [oʒurdɥi]
tomorrow	**demain** [dəmɛ̃]
the day after tomorrow	**après-demain** [aprɛdmɛ̃]

What day is it today?	**Quel jour sommes-nous aujourd'hui?** [kɛl ʒur sɔm-nu oʒurdɥi?]
It's …	**Nous sommes …** [nu sɔm …]
Monday	**lundi** [lœ̃di]
Tuesday	**mardi** [mardi]
Wednesday	**mercredi** [mɛrkrədi]

Thursday	**jeudi** [ʒødi]
Friday	**vendredi** [vɑ̃drədi]
Saturday	**samedi** [samdi]
Sunday	**dimanche** [dimɑ̃ʃ]

Greetings. Introductions

Hello.	**Bonjour.** [bɔ̃ʒuːr]
Pleased to meet you.	**Enchanté /Enchantée/** [ãʃãte]
Me too.	**Moi aussi.** [mwa osi]
I'd like you to meet ...	**Je voudrais vous présenter ...** [ʒə vudrɛ vu prezãte ...]
Nice to meet you.	**Ravi /Ravie/ de vous rencontrer.** [ravi də vu rãkõtre.]
How are you?	**Comment allez-vous?** [kɔmãtalevu?]
My name is ...	**Je m'appelle ...** [ʒə mapɛl ...]
His name is ...	**Il s'appelle ...** [il sapɛl ...]
Her name is ...	**Elle s'appelle ...** [ɛl sapɛl ...]
What's your name?	**Comment vous appelez-vous?** [kɔmã vuzaple-vu?]
What's his name?	**Quel est son nom?** [kɛl ɛ sõ nõ?]
What's her name?	**Quel est son nom?** [kɛl ɛ sõ nõ?]
What's your last name?	**Quel est votre nom de famille?** [kɛl ɛ vɔtr nõ də famij?]
You can call me ...	**Vous pouvez m'appeler ...** [vu puve maple ...]
Where are you from?	**D'où êtes-vous?** [du ɛt-vu?]
I'm from ...	**Je suis de ...** [ʒə sɥi də ...]
What do you do for a living?	**Qu'est-ce que vous faites dans la vie?** [kɛs kə vu fɛt dã la vi?]
Who is this?	**Qui est-ce?** [ki ɛs?]
Who is he?	**Qui est-il?** [ki ɛ-til?]
Who is she?	**Qui est-elle?** [ki ɛtɛl?]
Who are they?	**Qui sont-ils?** [ki sõ til?]

This is ...	**C'est ...**
	[sɛ ...]
my friend (masc.)	**mon ami**
	[mɔn ami]
my friend (fem.)	**mon amie**
	[mɔn ami]
my husband	**mon mari**
	[mɔ̃ mari]
my wife	**ma femme**
	[ma fam]

my father	**mon père**
	[mɔ̃ pɛr]
my mother	**ma mère**
	[ma mɛr]
my brother	**mon frère**
	[mɔ̃ frɛr]
my sister	**ma soeur**
	[ma sœr]
my son	**mon fils**
	[mɔ̃ fis]
my daughter	**ma fille**
	[ma fij]

This is our son.	**C'est notre fils.**
	[sɛ nɔtr fis]
This is our daughter.	**C'est notre fille.**
	[sɛ nɔtr fij]
These are my children.	**Ce sont mes enfants.**
	[sə sɔ̃ mezɑ̃fɑ̃]
These are our children.	**Ce sont nos enfants.**
	[sə sɔ̃ nozɑ̃fɑ̃]

Farewells

Good bye!	**Au revoir!** [o rəvwaːr!]
Bye! (inform.)	**Salut!** [saly!]
See you tomorrow.	**À demain.** [a dəmɛ̃]
See you soon.	**À bientôt.** [a bjɛ̃to]
See you at seven.	**On se revoit à sept heures.** [ɔ̃ sə rəvwa a sɛt œːr]

Have fun!	**Amusez-vous bien!** [amyze vu bjɛ̃!]
Talk to you later.	**On se voit plus tard.** [ɔ̃ sə vwa ply taːr]
Have a nice weekend.	**Bonne fin de semaine.** [bɔn fɛ̃ də səmɛn]
Good night.	**Bonne nuit.** [bɔn nɥi]

It's time for me to go.	**Il est l'heure que je parte.** [il ɛ lœr kə ʒə part]
I have to go.	**Je dois m'en aller.** [ʒə dwa mɑ̃nale]
I will be right back.	**Je reviens tout de suite.** [ʒə rəvjɛ̃ tu də sɥit]

It's late.	**Il est tard.** [il ɛ taːr]
I have to get up early.	**Je dois me lever tôt.** [ʒə dwa mə ləve to]
I'm leaving tomorrow.	**Je pars demain.** [ʒə par dəmɛ̃]
We're leaving tomorrow.	**Nous partons demain.** [nu partɔ̃ dəmɛ̃]

Have a nice trip!	**Bon voyage!** [bɔ̃ vwajaːʒ!]
It was nice meeting you.	**Enchanté de faire votre connaissance.** [ɑ̃ʃɑ̃te də fɛr votr kɔnɛsɑ̃s]
It was nice talking to you.	**Heureux /Heureuse/ d'avoir parlé avec vous.** [ørø /ørøz/ davwar parle avɛk vu]

Thanks for everything.	**Merci pour tout.** [mɛrsi pur tu]
I had a very good time.	**Je me suis vraiment amusé /amusée/** [ʒə mə sɥi vrɛmã amyze]
We had a very good time.	**Nous nous sommes vraiment amusés /amusées/** [nu nu sɔm vrɛmã amyze]

It was really great.	**C'était vraiment plaisant.** [setɛ vrɛmã plɛzã]
I'm going to miss you.	**Vous allez me manquer.** [vuzale mə mãke]
We're going to miss you.	**Vous allez nous manquer.** [vuzale nu mãke]

Good luck!	**Bonne chance!** [bɔn ʃã:s!]
Say hi to …	**Mes salutations à …** [me salytasjõ a …]

Foreign language

I don't understand.	**Je ne comprends pas.** [ʒə nə kɔ̃prɑ̃ pɑ]
Write it down, please.	**Écrivez-le, s'il vous plaît.** [ekrive lə, sil vu plɛ]
Do you speak ...?	**Parlez-vous ...?** [parle vu ...?]

I speak a little bit of ...	**Je parle un peu ...** [ʒə parl œ̃ pø ...]
English	**anglais** [ɑ̃glɛ]
Turkish	**turc** [tyrk]
Arabic	**arabe** [arab]
French	**français** [frɑ̃sɛ]

German	**allemand** [almɑ̃]
Italian	**italien** [italjɛ̃]
Spanish	**espagnol** [ɛspaɲɔl]
Portuguese	**portugais** [pɔrtygɛ]
Chinese	**chinois** [ʃinwa]
Japanese	**japonais** [ʒapɔnɛ]

Can you repeat that, please.	**Pouvez-vous le répéter, s'il vous plaît.** [puve vu lə repete, sil vu plɛ]
I understand.	**Je comprends.** [ʒə kɔ̃prɑ̃]
I don't understand.	**Je ne comprends pas.** [ʒə nə kɔ̃prɑ̃ pɑ]
Please speak more slowly.	**Parlez plus lentement, s'il vous plaît.** [parle ply lɑ̃tmɑ̃, sil vu plɛ]

Is that correct? (Am I saying it right?)	**Est-ce que c'est correct?** [ɛskə sɛ kɔrrɛkt?]
What is this? (What does this mean?)	**Qu'est-ce que c'est?** [kɛskə sɛ?]

Apologies

Excuse me, please.	**Excusez-moi, s'il vous plaît.** [ɛkskyze mwa, sil vu plɛ]
I'm sorry.	**Je suis désolé /désolée/** [ʒə sɥi dezɔle]
I'm really sorry.	**Je suis vraiment /désolée/** [ʒə sɥi vrɛmɑ̃ dezɔle]
Sorry, it's my fault.	**Désolé /Désolée/, c'est ma faute.** [dezɔle, sɛ ma fot]
My mistake.	**Au temps pour moi.** [otɑ̃ pur mwa]
May I ...?	**Puis-je ... ?** [pɥiʒ ...?]
Do you mind if I ...?	**Ça vous dérange si je ...?** [sa vu derɑ̃ʒ si ʒə ...?]
It's OK.	**Ce n'est pas grave.** [sə nɛ pɑ graːv]
It's all right.	**Ça va.** [sa va]
Don't worry about it.	**Ne vous inquiétez pas.** [nə vuzɛ̃kjete pɑ]

Agreement

Yes.	**Oui** [wi]
Yes, sure.	**Oui, bien sûr.** [wi, bjɛ̃ sy:r]
OK (Good!)	**Bien.** [bjɛ̃]
Very well.	**Très bien.** [trɛ bjɛ̃]
Certainly!	**Bien sûr!** [bjɛ̃sy:r!]
I agree.	**Je suis d'accord.** [ʒə sɥi dakɔ:r]

That's correct.	**C'est correct.** [sɛ kɔrrɛkt]
That's right.	**C'est exact.** [sɛtɛgzakt]
You're right.	**Vous avez raison.** [vuzave rɛzɔ̃]
I don't mind.	**Je ne suis pas contre.** [ʒə nə sɥi pɑ kɔ̃tr]
Absolutely right.	**Tout à fait correct.** [tutafɛ kɔrrɛkt]

It's possible.	**C'est possible.** [sɛ pɔsibl]
That's a good idea.	**C'est une bonne idée.** [sɛtyn bɔn ide]
I can't say no.	**Je ne peux pas dire non.** [ʒə nə pø pɑ dir nɔ̃]
I'd be happy to.	**J'en serai ravi /ravie/** [ʒɑ̃ səre ravi:]
With pleasure.	**Avec plaisir.** [avɛk plezi:r]

Refusal. Expressing doubt

No.	**Non**
	[nõ]
Certainly not.	**Absolument pas.**
	[absɔlymã pɑ]

I don't agree.	**Je ne suis pas d'accord.**
	[ʒə nə sɥi pɑ dakɔ:r]
I don't think so.	**Je ne le crois pas.**
	[ʒə nə lə krwa pɑ]
It's not true.	**Ce n'est pas vrai.**
	[sə nɛ pɑ vrɛ]

You are wrong.	**Vous avez tort.**
	[vuzave tɔ:r]
I think you are wrong.	**Je pense que vous avez tort.**
	[ʒə pãs kə vuzave tɔ:r]

I'm not sure.	**Je ne suis pas sûr /sûre/**
	[ʒə nə sɥi pɑ sy:r]
It's impossible.	**C'est impossible.**
	[sɛtɛ̃pɔsibl]
Nothing of the kind (sort)!	**Pas du tout!**
	[pɑ dy tu!]

The exact opposite.	**Au contraire!**
	[o kõtrɛ:r!]
I'm against it.	**Je suis contre.**
	[ʒə sɥi kõtr]
I don't care.	**Ça m'est égal.**
	[sa mɛ tegal]
I have no idea.	**Je n'ai aucune idée.**
	[ʒə ne okyn ide]
I doubt that.	**Je doute que cela soit ainsi.**
	[ʒə dut kə səla swa ɛ̃si]

Sorry, I can't.	**Désolé /Désolée/, je ne peux pas.**
	[dezɔle, ʒə nə pø pɑ]
Sorry, I don't want to.	**Désolé /Désolée/, je ne veux pas.**
	[dezɔle, ʒə nə vø pɑ]

Thank you, but I don't need this.	**Merci, mais ça ne m'intéresse pas.**
	[mɛrsi, mɛ sa nə mɛ̃terɛs pɑ]
It's late.	**Il se fait tard.**
	[il sə fɛ ta:r]

I have to get up early.	**Je dois me lever tôt.** [ʒə dwa mə ləve to]
I don't feel well.	**Je ne me sens pas bien.** [ʒə nə mə sɑ̃ pɑ bjɛ̃]

Expressing gratitude

Thank you.	**Merci.** [mɛrsi]
Thank you very much.	**Merci beaucoup.** [mɛrsi boku]
I really appreciate it.	**Je l'apprécie beaucoup.** [ʒə lapresi boku]
I'm really grateful to you.	**Je vous suis très reconnaissant.** [ʒə vu sɥi trɛ rəkɔnɛsɑ̃]
We are really grateful to you.	**Nous vous sommes très reconnaissant.** [nu vu sɔm trɛ rəkɔnɛsɑ̃]

Thank you for your time.	**Merci pour votre temps.** [mɛrsi pur vɔtr tɑ̃]
Thanks for everything.	**Merci pour tout.** [mɛrsi pur tu]
Thank you for ...	**Merci pour ...** [mɛrsi pur ...]
your help	**votre aide** [vɔtr ɛd]
a nice time	**les bons moments passés** [le bɔ̃ mɔmɑ̃ pɑse]

a wonderful meal	**un repas merveilleux** [œ̃ rəpɑ mɛrvɛjø]
a pleasant evening	**cette agréable soirée** [sɛt agreabl sware]
a wonderful day	**cette merveilleuse journée** [sɛt mɛrvɛjøz ʒurne]
an amazing journey	**une excursion extraordinaire** [yn ɛkskyrsjɔ̃ ɛkstraɔrdinɛr]

Don't mention it.	**Il n'y a pas de quoi.** [il njapɑ də kwa]
You are welcome.	**Je vous en prie.** [ʒə vuzɑ̃pri]
Any time.	**Mon plaisir.** [mɔ̃ plezi:r]
My pleasure.	**J'ai été heureux /heureuse/ de vous aider.** [ʒe ete ørø /ørøz/ də vuzɛde]

Forget it. It's alright.

Ça va. N'y pensez plus.
[sa va. ni pãse ply]

Don't worry about it.

Ne vous inquiétez pas.
[nə vuzĕkjete pɑ]

Congratulations. Best wishes

Congratulations!
Félicitations!
[felisitasjɔ̃!]

Happy birthday!
Joyeux anniversaire!
[ʒwajø zanivɛrsɛ:r!]

Merry Christmas!
Joyeux Noël!
[ʒwajø nɔɛl!]

Happy New Year!
Bonne Année!
[bɔn ane!]

Happy Easter!
Joyeuses Pâques!
[ʒwajøz pɑk!]

Happy Hanukkah!
Joyeux Hanoukka!
[ʒwajø anuka!]

I'd like to propose a toast.
Je voudrais proposer un toast.
[ʒə vudrɛ prɔpoze œ̃ tost]

Cheers!
Santé!
[sɑ̃te!]

Let's drink to ...!
Buvons à ...!
[byvɔ̃ a ...!]

To our success!
À notre succès!
[a nɔtr syksɛ!]

To your success!
À votre succès!
[a vɔtr syksɛ!]

Good luck!
Bonne chance!
[bɔn ʃɑ̃:s!]

Have a nice day!
Bonne journée!
[bɔn ʒurne!]

Have a good holiday!
Passez de bonnes vacances !
[pɑse də bɔn vakɑ̃s!]

Have a safe journey!
Bon voyage!
[bɔ̃ vwaja:ʒ!]

I hope you get better soon!
Rétablissez-vous vite.
[retablise-vu vit]

Socializing

Why are you sad?	**Pourquoi êtes-vous si triste?** [purkwa ɛt-vu si trist?]
Smile! Cheer up!	**Souriez!** [surje!]
Are you free tonight?	**Êtes-vous libre ce soir?** [ɛt-vu libr sə swaːr?]

May I offer you a drink?	**Puis-je vous offrir un verre?** [pɥiʒ vu zɔfrir œ̃ vɛːr?]
Would you like to dance?	**Voulez-vous danser?** [vule-vu dɑ̃se?]
Let's go to the movies.	**Et si on va au cinéma?** [e si ɔ̃va o sinema?]

May I invite you to ...?	**Puis-je vous inviter ...?** [pɥiʒ vu zɛ̃vite ...?]
a restaurant	**au restaurant** [o rɛstɔrɑ̃]
the movies	**au cinéma** [o sinema]
the theater	**au théâtre** [o teatr]
go for a walk	**pour une promenade** [pur yn prɔmnad]

At what time?	**À quelle heure?** [a kɛl œːr?]
tonight	**ce soir** [sə swar]
at six	**à six heures** [a siz œːr]
at seven	**à sept heures** [a sɛt œːr]
at eight	**à huit heures** [a ɥit œːr]
at nine	**à neuf heures** [a nœv œːr]

Do you like it here?	**Est-ce que vous aimez cet endroit?** [ɛskə vuzɛme sɛt ɑ̃drwa?]
Are you here with someone?	**Êtes-vous ici avec quelqu'un?** [ɛt-vu isi avɛk kelkœ̃?]
I'm with my friend.	**Je suis avec mon ami.** [ʒə sɥi avɛk mɔn ami]

I'm with my friends.	**Je suis avec mes amis.** [ʒə sɥi avɛk mezami]
No, I'm alone.	**Non, je suis seul /seule/** [nɔ̃, ʒə sɥi sœl]

Do you have a boyfriend?	**As-tu un copain?** [a ty œ̃ kɔpɛ̃?]
I have a boyfriend.	**J'ai un copain.** [ʒe œ̃ kɔpɛ̃]
Do you have a girlfriend?	**As-tu une copine?** [a ty yn kɔpin?]
I have a girlfriend.	**J'ai une copine.** [ʒe yn kɔpin]

Can I see you again?	**Est-ce que je peux te revoir?** [ɛskə ʒə pø tə rəvwa:r?]
Can I call you?	**Est-ce que je peux t'appeler?** [ɛskə ʒə pø taple?]
Call me. (Give me a call.)	**Appelle-moi.** [apɛl mwa]
What's your number?	**Quel est ton numéro?** [kɛl ɛ tɔ̃ nymero?]
I miss you.	**Tu me manques.** [ty mə mɑ̃:k]

You have a beautiful name.	**Vous avez un très beau nom.** [vuzave œ̃ trɛ bo nɔ̃]
I love you.	**Je t'aime.** [ʒə tɛm]
Will you marry me?	**Veux-tu te marier avec moi?** [vø-ty tə marje avɛk mwa?]
You're kidding!	**Vous plaisantez!** [vu plɛzɑ̃te!]
I'm just kidding.	**Je plaisante.** [ʒə plɛzɑ̃:t]

Are you serious?	**Êtes-vous sérieux /sérieuse/?** [ɛt-vu serjø /serjøz/?]
I'm serious.	**Je suis sérieux /sérieuse/** [ʒə sɥi serjø /serjøz/]
Really?!	**Vraiment?!** [vrɛmɑ̃?!]
It's unbelievable!	**C'est incroyable!** [sɛtɛ̃krwajabl!]
I don't believe you.	**Je ne vous crois pas.** [ʒə nə vu krwa pɑ]
I can't.	**Je ne peux pas.** [ʒə nə pø pɑ]
I don't know.	**Je ne sais pas.** [ʒə nə sɛ pɑ]
I don't understand you.	**Je ne vous comprends pas** [ʒə nə vu kɔ̃prɑ̃ pɑ]

Please go away.	**Laissez-moi! Allez-vous-en!**
	[lɛse-mwa! ale-vuzã!]
Leave me alone!	**Laissez-moi tranquille!**
	[lɛse-mwa trãkil!]

I can't stand him.	**Je ne le supporte pas.**
	[ʒə nə lə sypɔrt pa]
You are disgusting!	**Vous êtes dégoûtant!**
	[vuzɛt degutã!]
I'll call the police!	**Je vais appeler la police!**
	[ʒə ve aple la polis!]

Sharing impressions. Emotions

I like it.	**J'aime ça.** [ʒɛm sa]
Very nice.	**C'est gentil.** [sɛ ʒãti]
That's great!	**C'est super!** [sɛ sypɛr!]
It's not bad.	**C'est assez bien.** [sɛtase bjɛ̃]

I don't like it.	**Je n'aime pas ça.** [ʒə nɛm pɑ sa]
It's not good.	**Ce n'est pas bien.** [sə nɛ pɑ bjɛ̃]
It's bad.	**C'est mauvais.** [sɛ mɔvɛ]
It's very bad.	**Ce n'est pas bien du tout.** [sə nɛ pɑ bjɛ̃ dy tu]
It's disgusting.	**C'est dégoûtant.** [sɛ degutã]

I'm happy.	**Je suis content /contente/** [ʒə sɥi kõtã /kõtãt/]
I'm content.	**Je suis heureux /heureuse/** [ʒə sɥi ørø /ørøz/]
I'm in love.	**Je suis amoureux /amoureuse/** [ʒə sɥi amurø /amurøz/]
I'm calm.	**Je suis calme.** [ʒə sɥi kalm]
I'm bored.	**Je m'ennuie.** [ʒə mãnɥi]

I'm tired.	**Je suis fatigué /fatiguée/** [ʒə sɥi fatige]
I'm sad.	**Je suis triste.** [ʒə sɥi trist]
I'm frightened.	**J'ai peur.** [ʒe pœːr]

I'm angry.	**Je suis fâché /fâchée/** [ʒə sɥi faʃe]
I'm worried.	**Je suis inquiet /inquiète/** [ʒə sɥi ɛ̃kjɛ /ɛ̃kjɛt/]
I'm nervous.	**Je suis nerveux /nerveuse/** [ʒə sɥi nɛrvø /nɛrvøz/]

I'm jealous. (envious) **Je suis jaloux /jalouse/**
[ʒə sɥi ʒalu /ʒaluz/]

I'm surprised. **Je suis surpris /surprise/**
[ʒə sɥi syrpri /syrpriz/]

I'm perplexed. **Je suis gêné /gênée/**
[ʒə sɥi ʒɛne]

Problems. Accidents

I've got a problem.	**J'ai un problème.** [ʒe œ̃ prɔblɛm]
We've got a problem.	**Nous avons un problème.** [nuzavɔ̃ œ̃ prɔblɛm]
I'm lost.	**Je suis perdu /perdue/** [ʒə sɥi pɛrdy]
I missed the last bus (train).	**J'ai manqué le dernier bus (train).** [ʒe mɑ̃ke lə dɛrnje bys (trɛ̃)]
I don't have any money left.	**Je n'ai plus d'argent.** [ʒə ne ply darʒɑ̃]

I've lost my ...	**J'ai perdu mon ...** [ʒe pɛrdy mɔ̃ ...]
Someone stole my ...	**On m'a volé mon ...** [ɔ̃ ma vɔle mɔ̃ ...]
passport	**passeport** [paspɔ:r]
wallet	**portefeuille** [pɔrtəfœj]
papers	**papiers** [papje]
ticket	**billet** [bijɛ]

money	**argent** [arʒɑ̃]
handbag	**sac à main** [sak a mɛ̃]
camera	**appareil photo** [aparɛj fɔto]
laptop	**portable** [pɔrtabl]
tablet computer	**ma tablette** [ma tablɛt]
mobile phone	**mobile** [mɔbil]

Help me!	**Au secours!** [o səku:r!]
What's happened?	**Qu'est-il arrivé?** [kɛtil arive?]
fire	**un incendie** [œn ɛ̃sɑ̃di]

shooting	**des coups de feu** [de ku də fø]
murder	**un meurtre** [œ̃ mœrtr]
explosion	**une explosion** [yn ɛksplozjɔ̃]
fight	**une bagarre** [yn bagar]

Call the police!	**Appelez la police!** [aple la pɔlis!]
Please hurry up!	**Dépêchez-vous, s'il vous plaît!** [depɛʃe-vu, sil vu plɛ!]
I'm looking for the police station.	**Je cherche le commissariat de police.** [ʒə ʃɛrʃ lə kɔmisarja də pɔlis]
I need to make a call.	**Il me faut faire un appel.** [il mə fo fɛr œn apɛl]
May I use your phone?	**Puis-je utiliser votre téléphone?** [pɥiʒ ytilize vɔtr telefɔn?]

I've been ...	**J'ai été ...** [ʒe ete ...]
mugged	**agressé /agressée/** [agrɛse]
robbed	**volé /volée/** [vɔle]
raped	**violée** [vjɔle]
attacked (beaten up)	**attaqué /attaquée/** [atake]

Are you all right?	**Est-ce que ça va?** [ɛskə sa va?]
Did you see who it was?	**Avez-vous vu qui c'était?** [ave vu vy ki setɛ?]
Would you be able to recognize the person?	**Pourriez-vous reconnaître cette personne?** [purje-vu rəkɔnɛtr sɛt pɛrsɔn?]
Are you sure?	**Vous êtes sûr?** [vuzɛt sy:r?]

Please calm down.	**Calmez-vous, s'il vous plaît.** [kalme-vu, sil vu plɛ]
Take it easy!	**Calmez-vous!** [kalme-vu!]
Don't worry!	**Ne vous inquiétez pas.** [nə vuzɛ̃kjete pɑ]
Everything will be fine.	**Tout ira bien.** [tutira bjɛ̃]
Everything's all right.	**Ça va. Tout va bien.** [sa va. tu va bjɛ̃]

Come here, please.

Venez ici, s'il vous plaît.
[vəne isi, sil vu plε]

I have some questions for you.

J'ai des questions à vous poser.
[ʒe de kεstjɔ̃ a vu poze]

Wait a moment, please.

Attendez un moment, s'il vous plaît.
[atɑ̃de œ̃ mɔmɑ̃, sil vu plε]

Do you have any I.D.?

Avez-vous une carte d'identité?
[ave vu yn kart didɑ̃tite?]

Thanks. You can leave now.

Merci. Vous pouvez partir maintenant.
[mεrsi. vu puve partir mε̃tnɑ̃]

Hands behind your head!

Les mains derrière la tête!
[le mε̃ dεrjεr la tεt!]

You're under arrest!

Vous êtes arrêté!
[vuzεt arεte!]

Health problems

Please help me.	**Aidez-moi, s'il vous plaît.** [ɛde-mwa, sil vu plɛ]
I don't feel well.	**Je ne me sens pas bien.** [ʒə nə mə sã pɑ bjɛ̃]
My husband doesn't feel well.	**Mon mari ne se sent pas bien.** [mɔ̃ mari nə sə sã pɑ bjɛ̃]
My son ...	**Mon fils ...** [mɔ̃ fis ...]
My father ...	**Mon père ...** [mɔ̃ pɛr ...]
My wife doesn't feel well.	**Ma femme ne se sent pas bien.** [ma fam nə sə sã pɑ bjɛ̃]
My daughter ...	**Ma fille ...** [ma fij ...]
My mother ...	**Ma mère ...** [ma mɛr ...]
I've got a ...	**J'ai mal ...** [ʒe mal ...]
headache	**à la tête** [a la tɛt]
sore throat	**à la gorge** [a la gɔrʒ]
stomach ache	**à l'estomac** [a lɛstɔma]
toothache	**aux dents** [o dã]
I feel dizzy.	**J'ai le vertige.** [ʒe lə vɛrtiːʒ]
He has a fever.	**Il a de la fièvre.** [il a də la fjɛːvr]
She has a fever.	**Elle a de la fièvre.** [ɛl a də la fjɛːvr]
I can't breathe.	**Je ne peux pas respirer.** [ʒə nə pø pɑ rɛspire]
I'm short of breath.	**J'ai du mal à respirer.** [ʒe dy mal a rɛspire]
I am asthmatic.	**Je suis asthmatique.** [ʒə sɥi asmatik]
I am diabetic.	**Je suis diabétique.** [ʒə sɥi djabetik]

I can't sleep.	**Je ne peux pas dormir.**
	[ʒə nə pø pɑ dɔrmiːr]
food poisoning	**intoxication alimentaire**
	[ɛ̃tɔksikasjɔ̃ alimɑ̃tɛr]

It hurts here.	**Ça fait mal ici.**
	[sa fɛ mal isi]
Help me!	**Aidez-moi!**
	[ɛde-mwa!]
I am here!	**Je suis ici!**
	[ʒə sɥi isi!]
We are here!	**Nous sommes ici!**
	[nu sɔm isi!]
Get me out of here!	**Sortez-moi d'ici!**
	[sɔrte mwa disi!]
I need a doctor.	**J'ai besoin d'un docteur.**
	[ʒe bəzwɛ̃ dœ̃ dɔktœːr]
I can't move.	**Je ne peux pas bouger!**
	[ʒə nə pø pɑ buʒe!]
I can't move my legs.	**Je ne peux pas bouger mes jambes.**
	[ʒə nə pø pɑ buʒe me ʒɑ̃ːb]

I have a wound.	**Je suis blessé /blessée/**
	[ʒə sɥi blɛse]
Is it serious?	**Est-ce que c'est sérieux?**
	[ɛskə sɛ serjø?]
My documents are in my pocket.	**Mes papiers sont dans ma poche.**
	[me papje sɔ̃ dɑ̃ ma pɔʃ]
Calm down!	**Calmez-vous!**
	[kalme vu!]
May I use your phone?	**Puis-je utiliser votre téléphone?**
	[pɥiʒ ytilize vɔtr telefɔn?]

Call an ambulance!	**Appelez une ambulance!**
	[aple yn ɑ̃bylɑ̃ːs!]
It's urgent!	**C'est urgent!**
	[sɛtyrʒɑ̃!]
It's an emergency!	**C'est une urgence!**
	[sɛtyn yrʒɑ̃ːs!]
Please hurry up!	**Dépêchez-vous, s'il vous plaît!**
	[depɛʃe-vu, sil vu plɛ!]
Would you please call a doctor?	**Appelez le docteur, s'il vous plaît.**
	[aple lə dɔktœːr, sil vu plɛ]
Where is the hospital?	**Où est l'hôpital?**
	[u ɛ lɔpital?]

How are you feeling?	**Comment vous sentez-vous?**
	[kɔmɑ̃ vu sɑ̃te-vu?]
Are you all right?	**Est-ce que ça va?**
	[ɛskə sa va?]
What's happened?	**Qu'est-il arrivé?**
	[kɛtil arive?]

I feel better now.	**Je me sens mieux maintenant.** [ʒə mə sɑ̃ mjø mɛ̃tnɑ̃]
It's OK.	**Ça va. Tout va bien.** [sa va. tu va bjɛ̃]
It's all right.	**Ça va.** [sa va]

At the pharmacy

pharmacy (drugstore)

pharmacie
[farmasi]

24-hour pharmacy

pharmacie 24 heures
[farmasi vĕkatr œr]

Where is the closest pharmacy?

**Où se trouve la pharmacie
la plus proche?**
[u sə truv la farmasi
la ply prɔʃ?]

Is it open now?

Est-elle ouverte en ce moment?
[ɛtɛl uvɛrt ɑ̃ sə mɔmɑ̃?]

At what time does it open?

À quelle heure ouvre-t-elle?
[a kɛl œr uvr tɛl?]

At what time does it close?

à quelle heure ferme-t-elle?
[a kɛl œr fɛrm tɛl?]

Is it far?

C'est loin?
[sɛ lwɛ̃?]

Can I get there on foot?

Est-ce que je peux y aller à pied?
[ɛskə ʒə pø i ale a pje?]

Can you show me on the map?

**Pouvez-vous me le montrer
sur la carte?**
[puve vu mə lə mɔ̃tre
syr la kart?]

Please give me something for ...

**Pouvez-vous me donner
quelque chose contre ...**
[puve vu mə dɔne
kɛlkə ʃoz kɔ̃tr ...]

a headache

le mal de tête
[lə mal də tɛt]

a cough

la toux
[la tu]

a cold

le rhume
[lə rym]

the flu

la grippe
[la grip]

a fever

la fièvre
[la fjɛ:vr]

a stomach ache

un mal d'estomac
[œ̃ mal dɛstɔma]

nausea

la nausée
[la noze]

| diarrhea | la diarrhée
[la djare] |
| constipation | la constipation
[la kõstipasjõ] |

pain in the back	un mal de dos [œ̃ mal də do]
chest pain	les douleurs de poitrine [le dulœr də pwatrin]
side stitch	les points de côté [le pwɛ̃ də kote]
abdominal pain	les douleurs abdominales [le dulœr abdɔminal]

pill	une pilule [yn pilyl]
ointment, cream	un onguent, une crème [œn õgã, yn krɛm]
syrup	un sirop [œ̃ siro]
spray	un spray [œ̃ sprɛ]
drops	les gouttes [le gut]

You need to go to the hospital.	Vous devez allez à l'hôpital. [vu dəve ale a lɔpital]
health insurance	assurance maladie [asyrãs maladi]
prescription	prescription [prɛskripsjõ]
insect repellant	produit anti-insecte [prɔdµi ãti-ɛ̃sɛkt]
Band Aid	bandages adhésifs [bãdaʒ adezif]

The bare minimum

Excuse me, ...	**Excusez-moi, ...** [ɛkskyze mwa, ...]
Hello.	**Bonjour** [bɔ̃ʒuːr]
Thank you.	**Merci** [mɛrsi]
Good bye.	**Au revoir** [o rəvwaːr]
Yes.	**Oui** [wi]
No.	**Non** [nɔ̃]
I don't know.	**Je ne sais pas.** [ʒə nə sɛ pɑ]
Where? | Where to? | When?	**Où? | Où? | Quand?** [u? | u? | kɑ̃?]
I need ...	**J'ai besoin de ...** [ʒe bəzwɛ̃ də ...]
I want ...	**Je veux ...** [ʒə vø ...]
Do you have ...?	**Avez-vous ... ?** [ave vu ...?]
Is there a ... here?	**Est-ce qu'il y a ... ici?** [ɛs kilja ... isi?]
May I ...?	**Puis-je ... ?** [pɥiʒ ...?]
..., please (polite request)	**..., s'il vous plaît** [..., sil vu plɛ]
I'm looking for ...	**Je cherche ...** [ʒə ʃɛrʃ ...]
restroom	**les toilettes** [le twalɛt]
ATM	**un distributeur** [œ̃ distribytœːr]
pharmacy (drugstore)	**une pharmacie** [yn farmasi]
hospital	**l'hôpital** [lɔpital]
police station	**le commissariat de police** [lə kɔmisarja də polis]
subway	**une station de métro** [yn stasjɔ̃ də metro]

taxi	**un taxi** [œ̃ taksi]
train station	**la gare** [la gar]

My name is ...	**Je m'appelle ...** [ʒə mapɛl ...]
What's your name?	**Comment vous appelez-vous?** [kɔmɑ̃ vuzaple-vu?]
Could you please help me?	**Aidez-moi, s'il vous plaît.** [ɛde-mwa, sil vu plɛ]
I've got a problem.	**J'ai un problème.** [ʒe œ̃ prɔblɛm]
I don't feel well.	**Je ne me sens pas bien.** [ʒə nə mə sɑ̃ pɑ bjɛ̃]
Call an ambulance!	**Appelez une ambulance!** [aple yn ɑ̃bylɑ̃:s!]
May I make a call?	**Puis-je faire un appel?** [pɥiʒ fɛr œn apɛl?]

I'm sorry.	**Excusez-moi.** [ɛkskyze mwa]
You're welcome.	**Je vous en prie.** [ʒə vuzɑ̃pri]

I, me	**je, moi** [ʒə, mwa]
you (inform.)	**tu, toi** [ty, twa]
he	**il** [il]
she	**elle** [ɛl]
they (masc.)	**ils** [il]
they (fem.)	**elles** [ɛl]
we	**nous** [nu]
you (pl)	**vous** [vu]
you (sg, form.)	**Vous** [vu]

ENTRANCE	**ENTRÉE** [ɑ̃tre]
EXIT	**SORTIE** [sɔrti]
OUT OF ORDER	**HORS SERVICE | EN PANNE** [ɔr sɛrvis | ɑ̃ pan]
CLOSED	**FERMÉ** [fɛrme]

OPEN	**OUVERT**
	[uvɛr]
FOR WOMEN	**POUR LES FEMMES**
	[pur le fam]
FOR MEN	**POUR LES HOMMES**
	[pur le zɔm]

CONCISE DICTIONARY

This section contains more
than 1,500 useful words
arranged alphabetically.
The dictionary includes a lot
of gastronomic terms and
will be helpful when ordering
food at a restaurant or buying
groceries

T&P Books Publishing

DICTIONARY CONTENTS

T&P Books Publishing

time	**temps** (m)	[tã]
hour	**heure** (f)	[œr]
half an hour	**demi-heure** (f)	[dəmijœr]
minute	**minute** (f)	[minyt]
second	**seconde** (f)	[səgɔ̃d]
today (adv)	**aujourd'hui** (adv)	[oʒurdɥi]
tomorrow (adv)	**demain** (adv)	[dəmɛ̃]
yesterday (adv)	**hier** (adv)	[ijɛr]
Monday	**lundi** (m)	[lœ̃di]
Tuesday	**mardi** (m)	[mardi]
Wednesday	**mercredi** (m)	[mɛrkrədi]
Thursday	**jeudi** (m)	[ʒødi]
Friday	**vendredi** (m)	[vãdrədi]
Saturday	**samedi** (m)	[samdi]
Sunday	**dimanche** (m)	[dimãʃ]
day	**jour** (m)	[ʒur]
working day	**jour** (m) **ouvrable**	[ʒur uvrabl]
public holiday	**jour** (m) **férié**	[ʒur ferje]
weekend	**week-end** (m)	[wikɛnd]
week	**semaine** (f)	[səmɛn]
last week (adv)	**la semaine dernière**	[la səmɛn dɛrnjɛr]
next week (adv)	**la semaine prochaine**	[la səmɛn prɔʃɛn]
sunrise	**lever** (m) **du soleil**	[ləve dy sɔlɛj]
sunset	**coucher** (m) **du soleil**	[kuʃe dy sɔlɛj]
in the morning	**le matin**	[lə matɛ̃]
in the afternoon	**dans l'après-midi**	[dã laprɛmidi]
in the evening	**le soir**	[lə swar]
tonight (this evening)	**ce soir**	[sə swar]
at night	**la nuit**	[la nɥi]
midnight	**minuit** (f)	[minɥi]
January	**janvier** (m)	[ʒãvje]
February	**février** (m)	[fevrije]
March	**mars** (m)	[mars]
April	**avril** (m)	[avril]
May	**mai** (m)	[mɛ]
June	**juin** (m)	[ʒɥɛ̃]

July	juillet (m)	[ʒɥijɛ]
August	août (m)	[ut]
September	septembre (m)	[sɛparemã]
October	octobre (m)	[ɔktɔbr]
November	novembre (m)	[nɔvãbr]
December	décembre (m)	[desãbr]

in spring	au printemps	[oprɛ̃tã]
in summer	en été	[ɑn ete]
in fall	en automne	[ɑn otɔn]
in winter	en hiver	[ɑn ivɛr]

month	mois (m)	[mwa]
season (summer, etc.)	saison (f)	[sɛzɔ̃]
year	année (f)	[ane]
century	siècle (m)	[sjɛkl]

2. Numbers. Numerals

digit, figure	chiffre (m)	[ʃifr]
number	nombre (m)	[nɔ̃br]
minus sign	moins (m)	[mwɛ̃]
plus sign	plus (m)	[ply]
sum, total	somme (f)	[sɔm]

first (adj)	premier (adj)	[prəmje]
second (adj)	deuxième (adj)	[døzjɛm]
third (adj)	troisième (adj)	[trwazjɛm]

0 zero	zéro	[zero]
1 one	un	[œ̃]
2 two	deux	[dø]
3 three	trois	[trwa]
4 four	quatre	[katr]

5 five	cinq	[sɛ̃k]
6 six	six	[sis]
7 seven	sept	[sɛt]
8 eight	huit	[ɥit]
9 nine	neuf	[nœf]
10 ten	dix	[dis]

11 eleven	onze	[ɔ̃z]
12 twelve	douze	[duz]
13 thirteen	treize	[trɛz]
14 fourteen	quatorze	[katɔrz]
15 fifteen	quinze	[kɛ̃z]

| 16 sixteen | seize | [sɛz] |
| 17 seventeen | dix-sept | [disɛt] |

18 eighteen	dix-huit	[dizɥit]
19 nineteen	dix-neuf	[diznœf]
20 twenty	vingt	[vɛ̃]
30 thirty	trente	[trãt]
40 forty	quarante	[karãt]
50 fifty	cinquante	[sɛ̃kãt]
60 sixty	soixante	[swasãt]
70 seventy	soixante-dix	[swasãtdis]
80 eighty	quatre-vingts	[katrəvɛ̃]
90 ninety	quatre-vingt-dix	[katrəvɛ̃dis]
100 one hundred	cent	[sã]
200 two hundred	deux cents	[dø sã]
300 three hundred	trois cents	[trwa sã]
400 four hundred	quatre cents	[katr sã]
500 five hundred	cinq cents	[sɛ̃k sã]
600 six hundred	six cents	[si sã]
700 seven hundred	sept cents	[sɛt sã]
800 eight hundred	huit cents	[ɥi sã]
900 nine hundred	neuf cents	[nœf sã]
1000 one thousand	mille	[mil]
10000 ten thousand	dix mille	[di mil]
one hundred thousand	cent mille	[sã mil]
million	million (m)	[miljɔ̃]
billion	milliard (m)	[miljar]

3. Humans. Family

man (adult male)	homme (m)	[ɔm]
young man	jeune homme (m)	[ʒœn ɔm]
teenager	adolescent (m)	[adɔlesã]
woman	femme (f)	[fam]
girl (young woman)	jeune fille (f)	[ʒœn fij]
age	âge (m)	[ɑʒ]
adult (adj)	adulte (m)	[adylt]
middle-aged (adj)	d'âge moyen (adj)	[dɑʒ mwajɛ̃]
elderly (adj)	âgé (adj)	[ɑʒe]
old (adj)	vieux (adj)	[vjø]
old man	vieillard (m)	[vjɛjar]
old woman	vieille femme (f)	[vjɛj fam]
retirement	retraite (f)	[rətrɛt]
to retire (from job)	prendre sa retraite	[prãdr sa rətrɛt]
retiree	retraité (m)	[rətrɛte]

mother	**mère** (f)	[mɛr]
father	**père** (m)	[pɛr]
son	**fils** (m)	[fis]
daughter	**fille** (f)	[fij]
brother	**frère** (m)	[frɛr]
sister	**sœur** (f)	[sœr]

parents	**parents** (pl)	[parã]
child	**enfant** (m, f)	[ãfã]
children	**enfants** (pl)	[ãfã]
stepmother	**belle-mère, marâtre** (f)	[bɛlmɛr], [marɑtr]
stepfather	**beau-père** (m)	[bopɛr]

grandmother	**grand-mère** (f)	[grãmɛr]
grandfather	**grand-père** (m)	[grãpɛr]
grandson	**petit-fils** (m)	[pti fis]
granddaughter	**petite-fille** (f)	[ptit fij]
grandchildren	**petits-enfants** (pl)	[petizãfã]

uncle	**oncle** (m)	[ɔ̃kl]
aunt	**tante** (f)	[tãt]
nephew	**neveu** (m)	[nəvø]
niece	**nièce** (f)	[njɛs]

wife	**femme** (f)	[fam]
husband	**mari** (m)	[mari]
married (masc.)	**marié** (adj)	[marje]
married (fem.)	**mariée** (adj)	[marje]
widow	**veuve** (f)	[vœv]
widower	**veuf** (m)	[vœf]

| name (first name) | **prénom** (m) | [prenɔ̃] |
| surname (last name) | **nom** (m) **de famille** | [nɔ̃ də famij] |

relative	**parent** (m)	[parã]
friend (masc.)	**ami** (m)	[ami]
friendship	**amitié** (f)	[amitje]

partner	**partenaire** (m)	[partənɛr]
superior (n)	**supérieur** (m)	[syperjœr]
colleague	**collègue** (m, f)	[kɔlɛg]
neighbors	**voisins** (m pl)	[vwazɛ̃]

4. Human body

organism (body)	**organisme** (m)	[ɔrganism]
body	**corps** (m)	[kɔr]
heart	**cœur** (m)	[kœr]
blood	**sang** (m)	[sã]
brain	**cerveau** (m)	[sɛrvo]

nerve	nerf (m)	[nɛr]
bone	os (m)	[ɔs]
skeleton	squelette (f)	[skəlɛt]
spine (backbone)	colonne (f) vertébrale	[kɔlɔn vɛrtebral]
rib	côte (f)	[kot]
skull	crâne (m)	[kran]

muscle	muscle (m)	[myskl]
lungs	poumons (m pl)	[pumɔ̃]
skin	peau (f)	[po]

head	tête (f)	[tɛt]
face	visage (m)	[vizaʒ]
nose	nez (m)	[ne]
forehead	front (m)	[frɔ̃]
cheek	joue (f)	[ʒu]

mouth	bouche (f)	[buʃ]
tongue	langue (f)	[lɑ̃g]
tooth	dent (f)	[dɑ̃]
lips	lèvres (f pl)	[lɛvr]
chin	menton (m)	[mɑ̃tɔ̃]

ear	oreille (f)	[ɔrɛj]
neck	cou (m)	[ku]
throat	gorge (f)	[gɔrʒ]

eye	œil (m)	[œj]
pupil	pupille (f)	[pypij]
eyebrow	sourcil (m)	[sursi]
eyelash	cil (m)	[sil]

hair	cheveux (m pl)	[ʃəvø]
hairstyle	coiffure (f)	[kwafyr]
mustache	moustache (f)	[mustaʃ]
beard	barbe (f)	[barb]
to have (a beard, etc.)	porter (vt)	[pɔrte]
bald (adj)	chauve (adj)	[ʃov]

hand	main (f)	[mɛ̃]
arm	bras (m)	[bra]
finger	doigt (m)	[dwa]
nail	ongle (m)	[ɔ̃gl]
palm	paume (f)	[pom]

shoulder	épaule (f)	[epol]
leg	jambe (f)	[ʒɑ̃b]
foot	pied (m)	[pje]
knee	genou (m)	[ʒənu]
heel	talon (m)	[talɔ̃]
back	dos (m)	[do]
waist	taille (f)	[taj]

beauty mark	grain (m) de beauté	[grɛ̃ də bote]
birthmark	tache (f) de vin	[taʃ də vɛ̃]
(café au lait spot)		

5. Medicine. Diseases. Drugs

health	santé (f)	[sɑ̃te]
well (not sick)	en bonne santé	[ɑ̃ bɔn sɑ̃te]
sickness	maladie (f)	[maladi]
to be sick	être malade	[ɛtr malad]
ill, sick (adj)	malade (adj)	[malad]

cold (illness)	refroidissement (m)	[rəfrwadismɑ̃]
to catch a cold	prendre froid	[prɑ̃dr frwa]
tonsillitis	angine (f)	[ɑ̃ʒin]
pneumonia	pneumonie (f)	[pnømɔni]
flu, influenza	grippe (f)	[grip]

runny nose (coryza)	rhume (m)	[rym]
cough	toux (f)	[tu]
to cough (vi)	tousser (vi)	[tuse]
to sneeze (vi)	éternuer (vi)	[etɛrnɥe]

stroke	insulte (f)	[ɛ̃sylt]
heart attack	crise (f) cardiaque	[kriz kardjak]
allergy	allergie (f)	[alɛrʒi]
asthma	asthme (m)	[asm]
diabetes	diabète (m)	[djabɛt]

tumor	tumeur (f)	[tymœr]
cancer	cancer (m)	[kɑ̃sɛr]
alcoholism	alcoolisme (m)	[alkɔlism]
AIDS	SIDA (m)	[sida]
fever	fièvre (f)	[fjɛvr]
seasickness	mal (m) de mer	[mal də mɛr]

bruise (hématome)	bleu (m)	[blø]
bump (lump)	bosse (f)	[bɔs]
to limp (vi)	boiter (vi)	[bwate]
dislocation	foulure (f)	[fulyr]
to dislocate (vt)	se démettre (vp)	[sə demɛtr]

fracture	fracture (f)	[fraktyr]
burn (injury)	brûlure (f)	[brylyr]
injury	blessure (f)	[blesyr]
pain	douleur (f)	[dulœr]
toothache	mal (m) de dents	[mal də dɑ̃]

| to sweat (perspire) | suer (vi) | [sɥe] |
| deaf (adj) | sourd (adj) | [sur] |

mute (adj)	muet (adj)	[mɥɛ]
immunity	immunité (f)	[imynite]
virus	virus (m)	[virys]
microbe	microbe (m)	[mikrɔb]
bacterium	bactérie (f)	[bakteri]
infection	infection (f)	[ɛ̃fɛksjɔ̃]
hospital	hôpital (m)	[ɔpital]
cure	cure (f)	[kyr]
to vaccinate (vt)	vacciner (vt)	[vaksine]
to be in a coma	être dans le coma	[ɛtr dɑ̃ lə kɔma]
intensive care	réanimation (f)	[reanimasjɔ̃]
symptom	symptôme (m)	[sɛ̃ptom]
pulse	pouls (m)	[pu]

6. Feelings. Emotions. Conversation

I, me	je	[ʒə]
you	tu	[ty]
he	il	[il]
she	elle	[ɛl]
it	ça	[sa]
we	nous	[nu]
you (to a group)	vous	[vu]
they (masc.)	ils	[il]
they (fem.)	elles	[ɛl]
Hello! (fam.)	Bonjour!	[bɔ̃ʒur]
Hello! (form.)	Bonjour!	[bɔ̃ʒur]
Good morning!	Bonjour!	[bɔ̃ʒur]
Good afternoon!	Bonjour!	[bɔ̃ʒur]
Good evening!	Bonsoir!	[bɔ̃swar]
to say hello	dire bonjour	[dir bɔ̃ʒur]
to greet (vt)	saluer (vt)	[salɥe]
How are you? (form.)	Comment allez-vous?	[kɔmɑ̃talevu]
How are you? (fam.)	Comment ça va?	[kɔmɑ̃ sa va]
Bye-Bye! Goodbye!	Au revoir!	[orevwar]
Thank you!	Merci!	[mɛrsi]
feelings	sentiments (m pl)	[sɑ̃timɑ̃]
to be hungry	avoir faim	[avwar fɛ̃]
to be thirsty	avoir soif	[avwar swaf]
tired (adj)	fatigué (adj)	[fatige]
to be worried	s'inquiéter (vp)	[sɛ̃kjete]
to be nervous	s'énerver (vp)	[senɛrve]
hope	espoir (m)	[ɛspwar]
to hope (vi, vt)	espérer (vi)	[ɛspere]

character	caractère (m)	[karaktɛr]
modest (adj)	modeste (adj)	[mɔdɛst]
lazy (adj)	paresseux (adj)	[parɛsø]
generous (adj)	généreux (adj)	[ʒenerø]
talented (adj)	doué (adj)	[dwe]

honest (adj)	honnête (adj)	[ɔnɛt]
serious (adj)	sérieux (adj)	[serjø]
shy, timid (adj)	timide (adj)	[timid]
sincere (adj)	sincère (adj)	[sɛ̃sɛr]
coward	peureux (m)	[pœrø]

to sleep (vi)	dormir (vi)	[dɔrmir]
dream	rêve (m)	[rɛv]
bed	lit (m)	[li]
pillow	oreiller (m)	[ɔrɛje]

insomnia	insomnie (f)	[ɛ̃sɔmni]
to go to bed	aller se coucher	[ale sə kuʃe]
nightmare	cauchemar (m)	[koʃmar]
alarm clock	réveil (m)	[revɛj]

smile	sourire (m)	[surir]
to smile (vi)	sourire (vi)	[surir]
to laugh (vi)	rire (vi)	[rir]

quarrel	dispute (f)	[dispyt]
insult	insulte (f)	[ɛ̃sylt]
resentment	offense (f)	[ɔfɑ̃s]
angry (mad)	fâché (adj)	[faʃe]

7. Clothing. Personal accessories

clothes	vêtement (m)	[vɛtmɑ̃]
coat (overcoat)	manteau (m)	[mɑ̃to]
fur coat	manteau (m) de fourrure	[mɑ̃to də furyr]
jacket (e.g., leather ~)	veste (f)	[vɛst]
raincoat (trenchcoat, etc.)	imperméable (m)	[ɛ̃pɛrmeabl]

shirt (button shirt)	chemise (f)	[ʃəmiz]
pants	pantalon (m)	[pɑ̃talɔ̃]
suit jacket	veston (m)	[vɛstɔ̃]
suit	complet (m)	[kɔ̃plɛ]

dress (frock)	robe (f)	[rɔb]
skirt	jupe (f)	[ʒyp]
T-shirt	tee-shirt (m)	[tiʃœrt]
bathrobe	peignoir (m) de bain	[pɛɲwar də bɛ̃]
pajamas	pyjama (m)	[piʒama]
workwear	tenue (f) de travail	[təny də travaj]

underwear	sous-vêtements (m pl)	[suvɛtmɑ̃]
socks	chaussettes (f pl)	[ʃosɛt]
bra	soutien-gorge (m)	[sutjɛ̃gɔrʒ]
pantyhose	collants (m pl)	[kɔlɑ̃]
stockings (thigh highs)	bas (m pl)	[ba]
bathing suit	maillot (m) de bain	[majo də bɛ̃]
hat	chapeau (m)	[ʃapo]
footwear	chaussures (f pl)	[ʃosyr]
boots (cowboy ~)	bottes (f pl)	[bɔt]
heel	talon (m)	[talɔ̃]
shoestring	lacet (m)	[lase]
shoe polish	cirage (m)	[siraʒ]
cotton (n)	coton (m)	[kɔtɔ̃]
wool (n)	laine (f)	[lɛn]
fur (n)	fourrure (f)	[furyr]
gloves	gants (m pl)	[gɑ̃]
mittens	moufles (f pl)	[mufl]
scarf (muffler)	écharpe (f)	[eʃarp]
glasses (eyeglasses)	lunettes (f pl)	[lynɛt]
umbrella	parapluie (m)	[paraplɥi]
tie (necktie)	cravate (f)	[kravat]
handkerchief	mouchoir (m)	[muʃwar]
comb	peigne (m)	[pɛɲ]
hairbrush	brosse (f) à cheveux	[brɔs ɑ ʃəvø]
buckle	boucle (f)	[bukl]
belt	ceinture (f)	[sɛ̃tyr]
purse	sac (m) à main	[sak ɑ mɛ̃]
collar	col (m)	[kɔl]
pocket	poche (f)	[pɔʃ]
sleeve	manche (f)	[mɑ̃ʃ]
fly (on trousers)	braguette (f)	[bragɛt]
zipper (fastener)	fermeture (f) à glissière	[fɛrmətyr ɑ glisjɛr]
button	bouton (m)	[butɔ̃]
to get dirty (vi)	se salir (vp)	[sə salir]
stain (mark, spot)	tache (f)	[taʃ]

8. City. Urban institutions

store	magasin (m)	[magazɛ̃]
shopping mall	centre (m) commercial	[sɑ̃tr kɔmɛrsjal]
supermarket	supermarché (m)	[sypɛrmarʃe]
shoe store	magasin (m) de chaussures	[magazɛ̃ də ʃosyr]

bookstore	librairie (f)	[librɛri]
drugstore, pharmacy	pharmacie (f)	[farmasi]
bakery	boulangerie (f)	[bulɑ̃ʒri]
candy store	pâtisserie (f)	[pɑtisri]
grocery store	épicerie (f)	[episri]
butcher shop	boucherie (f)	[buʃri]
produce store	magasin (m) de légumes	[magazɛ̃ də legym]
market	marché (m)	[marʃe]

hair salon	salon (m) de coiffure	[salɔ̃ də kwafyr]
post office	poste (f)	[pɔst]
dry cleaners	pressing (m)	[presiŋ]
circus	cirque (m)	[sirk]
zoo	zoo (m)	[zoo]

theater	théâtre (m)	[teɑtr]
movie theater	cinéma (m)	[sinema]
museum	musée (m)	[myze]
library	bibliothèque (f)	[biblijɔtɛk]

mosque	mosquée (f)	[mɔske]
synagogue	synagogue (f)	[sinagɔg]
cathedral	cathédrale (f)	[katedral]
temple	temple (m)	[tɑ̃pl]
church	église (f)	[egliz]

college	institut (m)	[ɛ̃stity]
university	université (f)	[ynivɛrsite]
school	école (f)	[ekɔl]

hotel	hôtel (m)	[otɛl]
bank	banque (f)	[bɑ̃k]
embassy	ambassade (f)	[ɑ̃basad]
travel agency	agence (f) de voyages	[aʒɑ̃s də vwajaʒ]

subway	métro (m)	[metro]
hospital	hôpital (m)	[ɔpital]
gas station	station-service (f)	[stasjɔ̃sɛrvis]
parking lot	parking (m)	[parkiŋ]

ENTRANCE	ENTRÉE	[ɑ̃tre]
EXIT	SORTIE	[sɔrti]
PUSH	POUSSER	[puse]
PULL	TIRER	[tire]
OPEN	OUVERT	[uvɛr]
CLOSED	FERMÉ	[fɛrme]

monument	monument (m)	[mɔnymɑ̃]
fortress	forteresse (f)	[fɔrtərɛs]
palace	palais (m)	[palɛ]
medieval (adj)	médiéval (adj)	[medjeval]
ancient (adj)	ancien (adj)	[ɑ̃sjɛ̃]

| national (adj) | national (adj) | [nasjɔnal] |
| well-known (adj) | connu (adj) | [kɔny] |

9. Money. Finances

money	argent (m)	[arʒɑ̃]
coin	monnaie (f)	[mɔnɛ]
dollar	dollar (m)	[dɔlar]
euro	euro (m)	[øro]

ATM	distributeur (m)	[distribytœr]
currency exchange	bureau (m) de change	[byro də ʃɑ̃ʒ]
exchange rate	cours (m) de change	[kur də ʃɑ̃ʒ]
cash	espèces (f pl)	[ɛspɛs]

How much?	Combien?	[kɔ̃bjɛ̃]
to pay (vi, vt)	payer (vi, vt)	[peje]
payment	paiement (m)	[pɛmɑ̃]
change (give the ~)	monnaie (f)	[mɔnɛ]

price	prix (m)	[pri]
discount	rabais (m)	[rabɛ]
cheap (adj)	bon marché (adj)	[bɔ̃ marʃe]
expensive (adj)	cher (adj)	[ʃɛr]

bank	banque (f)	[bɑ̃k]
account	compte (m)	[kɔ̃t]
credit card	carte (f) de crédit	[kart də kredi]
check	chèque (m)	[ʃɛk]
to write a check	faire un chèque	[fɛr œ̃ ʃɛk]
checkbook	chéquier (m)	[ʃekje]

debt	dette (f)	[dɛt]
debtor	débiteur (m)	[debitœr]
to lend (money)	prêter (vt)	[prete]
to borrow (vi, vt)	emprunter (vt)	[ɑ̃prœ̃te]

to rent (~ a tuxedo)	louer (vt)	[lwe]
on credit (adv)	à crédit (adv)	[akredi]
wallet	portefeuille (m)	[portəfœj]
safe	coffre fort (m)	[kɔfr fɔr]
inheritance	héritage (m)	[eritaʒ]
fortune (wealth)	fortune (f)	[fɔrtyn]

tax	impôt (m)	[ɛ̃po]
fine	amende (f)	[amɑ̃d]
to fine (vt)	mettre une amende	[mɛtr ynamɑ̃d]

| wholesale (adj) | en gros (adj) | [ɑ̃ gro] |
| retail (adj) | au détail (adj) | [odetaj] |

to insure (vt)	**assurer** (vt)	[asyre]
insurance	**assurance** (f)	[asyrɑ̃s]
capital	**capital** (m)	[kapital]
turnover	**chiffre** (m) **d'affaires**	[ʃifr dafɛr]
stock (share)	**action** (f)	[aksjɔ̃]
profit	**profit** (m)	[prɔfi]
profitable (adj)	**profitable** (adj)	[prɔfitabl]
crisis	**crise** (f)	[kriz]
bankruptcy	**faillite** (f)	[fajit]
to go bankrupt	**faire faillite**	[fɛr fajit]
accountant	**comptable** (m)	[kɔ̃tabl]
salary	**salaire** (m)	[salɛr]
bonus (money)	**prime** (f)	[prim]

10. Transportation

bus	**autobus** (m)	[otobys]
streetcar	**tramway** (m)	[tramwɛ]
trolley bus	**trolleybus** (m)	[trɔlɛbys]
to go by ...	**prendre ...**	[prɑ̃dr]
to get on (~ the bus)	**monter** (vi)	[mɔ̃te]
to get off ...	**descendre de ...**	[desɑ̃dr də]
stop (e.g., bus ~)	**arrêt** (m)	[arɛ]
terminus	**terminus** (m)	[tɛrminys]
schedule	**horaire** (m)	[ɔrɛr]
ticket	**ticket** (m)	[tikɛ]
to be late (for ...)	**être en retard**	[ɛtr ɑ̃ rətar]
taxi, cab	**taxi** (m)	[taksi]
by taxi	**en taxi**	[ɑ̃ taksi]
taxi stand	**arrêt** (m) **de taxi**	[arɛ də taksi]
traffic	**trafic** (m)	[trafik]
rush hour	**heures** (f pl) **de pointe**	[œr də pwɛ̃t]
to park (vi)	**se garer** (vp)	[sə gare]
subway	**métro** (m)	[metro]
station	**station** (f)	[stasjɔ̃]
train	**train** (m)	[trɛ̃]
train station	**gare** (f)	[gar]
rails	**rails** (m pl)	[raj]
compartment	**compartiment** (m)	[kɔ̃partimɑ̃]
berth	**couchette** (f)	[kuʃɛt]
airplane	**avion** (m)	[avjɔ̃]
air ticket	**billet** (m) **d'avion**	[bijɛ davjɔ̃]

airline	compagnie (f) aérienne	[kɔ̃paɲi aerjɛn]
airport	aéroport (m)	[aeropor]
flight (act of flying)	vol (m)	[vɔl]
luggage	bagage (m)	[bagaʒ]
luggage cart	chariot (m)	[ʃarjo]
ship	bateau (m)	[bato]
cruise ship	bateau (m) de croisière	[bato də krwazjɛr]
yacht	yacht (m)	[jot]
boat (flat-bottomed ~)	canot (m) à rames	[kano ɑ ram]
captain	capitaine (m)	[kapitɛn]
cabin	cabine (f)	[kabin]
port (harbor)	port (m)	[pɔr]
bicycle	vélo (m)	[velo]
scooter	scooter (m)	[skutœr]
motorcycle, bike	moto (f)	[moto]
pedal	pédale (f)	[pedal]
pump	pompe (f)	[pɔ̃p]
wheel	roue (f)	[ru]
automobile, car	automobile (f)	[otomobil]
ambulance	ambulance (f)	[ãbylãs]
truck	camion (m)	[kamjɔ̃]
used (adj)	d'occasion (adj)	[dɔkazjɔ̃]
car crash	accident (m)	[aksidã]
repair	réparation (f)	[reparasjɔ̃]

11. Food. Part 1

meat	viande (f)	[vjãd]
chicken	poulet (m)	[pulɛ]
duck	canard (m)	[kanar]
pork	du porc	[dy pɔr]
veal	du veau	[dy vo]
lamb	du mouton	[dy mutɔ̃]
beef	du bœuf	[dy bœf]
sausage (bologna, pepperoni, etc.)	saucisson (m)	[sosisɔ̃]
egg	œuf (m)	[œf]
fish	poisson (m)	[pwasɔ̃]
cheese	fromage (m)	[frɔmaʒ]
sugar	sucre (m)	[sykr]
salt	sel (m)	[sɛl]
rice	riz (m)	[ri]
pasta	pâtes (m pl)	[pɑt]

butter	beurre (m)	[bœr]
vegetable oil	huile (f) végétale	[ɥil veʒetal]
bread	pain (m)	[pɛ̃]
chocolate (n)	chocolat (m)	[ʃɔkɔla]

wine	vin (m)	[vɛ̃]
coffee	café (m)	[kafe]
milk	lait (m)	[lɛ]
juice	jus (m)	[ʒy]
beer	bière (f)	[bjɛr]
tea	thé (m)	[te]

tomato	tomate (f)	[tɔmat]
cucumber	concombre (m)	[kɔ̃kɔ̃br]
carrot	carotte (f)	[karɔt]
potato	pomme (f) de terre	[pɔm də tɛr]
onion	oignon (m)	[ɔɲɔ̃]
garlic	ail (m)	[aj]

cabbage	chou (m)	[ʃu]
beetroot	betterave (f)	[bɛtrav]
eggplant	aubergine (f)	[obɛrʒin]
dill	fenouil (m)	[fənuj]
lettuce	laitue (f), salade (f)	[lety], [salad]
corn (maize)	maïs (m)	[mais]

fruit	fruit (m)	[frɥi]
apple	pomme (f)	[pɔm]
pear	poire (f)	[pwar]
lemon	citron (m)	[sitrɔ̃]
orange	orange (f)	[ɔrɑ̃ʒ]
strawberry	fraise (f)	[frɛz]

plum	prune (f)	[pryn]
raspberry	framboise (f)	[frɑ̃bwaz]
pineapple	ananas (m)	[anana]
banana	banane (f)	[banan]
watermelon	pastèque (f)	[pastɛk]
grape	raisin (m)	[rɛzɛ̃]
melon	melon (m)	[məlɔ̃]

12. Food. Part 2

cuisine	cuisine (f)	[kɥizin]
recipe	recette (f)	[rəsɛt]
food	nourriture (f)	[nurityr]

to have breakfast	prendre le petit déjeuner	[prɑ̃dr ləpti deʒœne]
to have lunch	déjeuner (vi)	[deʒœne]
to have dinner	dîner (vi)	[dine]

taste, flavor	goût (m)	[gu]
tasty (adj)	bon (adj)	[bɔ̃]
cold (adj)	froid (adj)	[frwa]
hot (adj)	chaud (adj)	[ʃo]
sweet (sugary)	sucré (adj)	[sykre]
salty (adj)	salé (adj)	[sale]

sandwich (bread)	sandwich (m)	[sãdwitʃ]
side dish	garniture (f)	[garnityr]
filling (for cake, pie)	garniture (f)	[garnityr]
sauce	sauce (f)	[sos]
piece (of cake, pie)	morceau (m)	[mɔrso]

diet	régime (m)	[reʒim]
vitamin	vitamine (f)	[vitamin]
calorie	calorie (f)	[kalori]
vegetarian (n)	végétarien (m)	[veʒetarjɛ̃]

restaurant	restaurant (m)	[rɛstɔrã]
coffee house	salon (m) de café	[salɔ̃ də kafe]
appetite	appétit (m)	[apeti]
Enjoy your meal!	Bon appétit!	[bɔn apeti]

waiter	serveur (m)	[sɛrvœr]
waitress	serveuse (f)	[sɛrvøz]
bartender	barman (m)	[barman]
menu	carte (f)	[kart]

spoon	cuillère (f)	[kɥijɛr]
knife	couteau (m)	[kuto]
fork	fourchette (f)	[furʃɛt]
cup (e.g., coffee ~)	tasse (f)	[tɑs]

plate (dinner ~)	assiette (f)	[asjɛt]
saucer	soucoupe (f)	[sukup]
napkin (on table)	serviette (f)	[sɛrvjɛt]
toothpick	cure-dent (m)	[kyrdã]

to order (meal)	commander (vt)	[kɔmãde]
course, dish	plat (m)	[pla]
portion	portion (f)	[pɔrsjɔ̃]
appetizer	hors-d'œuvre (m)	[ɔrdœvr]
salad	salade (f)	[salad]
soup	soupe (f)	[sup]

dessert	dessert (m)	[desɛr]
whole fruit jam	confiture (f)	[kɔ̃fityr]
ice-cream	glace (f)	[glas]

check	addition (f)	[adisjɔ̃]
to pay the check	régler l'addition	[regle ladisjɔ̃]
tip	pourboire (m)	[purbwar]

13. House. Apartment. Part 1

house	**maison** (f)	[mɛzɔ̃]
country house	**maison** (f) **de campagne**	[mɛzɔ̃ də kɑ̃paɲ]
villa (seaside ~)	**villa** (f)	[vila]
floor, story	**étage** (m)	[etaʒ]
entrance	**entrée** (f)	[ɑ̃tre]
wall	**mur** (m)	[myr]
roof	**toit** (m)	[twa]
chimney	**cheminée** (f)	[ʃəmine]
attic (storage place)	**grenier** (m)	[grənje]
window	**fenêtre** (f)	[fənɛtr]
window ledge	**rebord** (m)	[rəbɔr]
balcony	**balcon** (m)	[balkɔ̃]
stairs (stairway)	**escalier** (m)	[ɛskalje]
mailbox	**boîte** (f) **à lettres**	[bwat ɑ lɛtr]
garbage can	**poubelle** (f)	[pubɛl]
elevator	**ascenseur** (m)	[asɑ̃sœr]
electricity	**électricité** (f)	[elɛktrisite]
light bulb	**ampoule** (f)	[ɑ̃pul]
switch	**interrupteur** (m)	[ɛ̃teryptœr]
wall socket	**prise** (f)	[priz]
fuse	**fusible** (m)	[fyzibl]
door	**porte** (f)	[pɔrt]
handle, doorknob	**poignée** (f)	[pwaɲe]
key	**clé, clef** (f)	[kle]
doormat	**paillasson** (m)	[pajasɔ̃]
door lock	**serrure** (f)	[seryr]
doorbell	**sonnette** (f)	[sɔnɛt]
knock (at the door)	**coups** (m pl) **à la porte**	[ku ɑla pɔrt]
to knock (vi)	**frapper** (vi)	[frape]
peephole	**judas** (m)	[ʒyda]
yard	**cour** (f)	[kur]
garden	**jardin** (m)	[ʒardɛ̃]
swimming pool	**piscine** (f)	[pisin]
gym (home gym)	**salle** (f) **de gym**	[sal də ʒim]
tennis court	**court** (m) **de tennis**	[kur də tenis]
garage	**garage** (m)	[garaʒ]
private property	**propriété** (f) **privée**	[prɔprijete prive]
warning sign	**panneau** (m) **d'avertissement**	[pano davɛrtismɑ̃]
security	**sécurité** (f)	[sekyrite]
security guard	**agent** (m) **de sécurité**	[aʒɑ̃ də sekyrite]

renovations	rénovation (f)	[renɔvasjɔ̃]
to renovate (vt)	faire la rénovation	[fɛr la renɔvasjɔ̃]
to put in order	remettre en ordre	[rəmɛtr anɔrdr]
to paint (~ a wall)	peindre (vt)	[pɛ̃dr]
wallpaper	papier (m) peint	[papje pɛ̃]
to varnish (vt)	vernir (vt)	[vɛrnir]

pipe	tuyau (m)	[tyijo]
tools	outils (m pl)	[uti]
basement	sous-sol (m)	[susɔl]
sewerage (system)	égouts (m pl)	[egu]

14. House. Apartment. Part 2

apartment	appartement (m)	[apartəmɑ̃]
room	chambre (f)	[ʃɑ̃br]
bedroom	chambre (f) à coucher	[ʃɑ̃br a kuʃe]
dining room	salle (f) à manger	[sal a mɑ̃ʒe]

living room	salon (m)	[salɔ̃]
study (home office)	bureau (m)	[byro]
entry room	antichambre (f)	[ɑ̃tiʃɑ̃br]
bathroom (room with a bath or shower)	salle (f) de bains	[sal də bɛ̃]
half bath	toilettes (f pl)	[twalɛt]

| floor | plancher (m) | [plɑ̃ʃe] |
| ceiling | plafond (m) | [plafɔ̃] |

to dust (vt)	essuyer la poussière	[esyije la pusjɛr]
vacuum cleaner	aspirateur (m)	[aspiratœr]
to vacuum (vt)	passer l'aspirateur	[pɑse laspiratœr]

mop	balai (m) à franges	[balɛ a frɑ̃ʒ]
dust cloth	torchon (m)	[tɔrʃɔ̃]
short broom	balayette (f)	[balɛjɛt]
dustpan	pelle (f) à ordures	[pɛl a ɔrdyr]

furniture	meubles (m pl)	[mœbl]
table	table (f)	[tabl]
chair	chaise (f)	[ʃɛz]
armchair	fauteuil (m)	[fotœj]

bookcase	bibliothèque (f)	[biblijɔtɛk]
shelf	rayon (m)	[rɛjɔ̃]
wardrobe	armoire (f)	[armwar]

mirror	miroir (m)	[mirwar]
carpet	tapis (m)	[tapi]
fireplace	cheminée (f)	[ʃəmine]

drapes	rideaux (m pl)	[rido]
table lamp	lampe (f) de table	[lɑ̃p də tabl]
chandelier	lustre (m)	[lystr]
kitchen	cuisine (f)	[kɥizin]
gas stove (range)	cuisinière (f) à gaz	[kɥizinjɛr ɑ gaz]
electric stove	cuisinière (f) électrique	[kɥizinjɛr elɛktrik]
microwave oven	four (m) micro-ondes	[fur mikrɔ̃d]
refrigerator	réfrigérateur (m)	[refriʒeratœr]
freezer	congélateur (m)	[kɔ̃ʒelatœr]
dishwasher	lave-vaisselle (m)	[lavvesɛl]
faucet	robinet (m)	[rɔbinɛ]
meat grinder	hachoir (m)	[aʃwar]
juicer	centrifugeuse (f)	[sɑ̃trifyʒøz]
toaster	grille-pain (m)	[grijpɛ̃]
mixer	batteur (m)	[batœr]
coffee machine	machine (f) à café	[maʃin ɑ kafe]
kettle	bouilloire (f)	[bujwar]
teapot	théière (f)	[tejɛr]
TV set	télé (f)	[tele]
VCR (video recorder)	magnétoscope (m)	[maɲetɔskɔp]
iron (e.g., steam ~)	fer (m) à repasser	[fɛr ɑ rəpase]
telephone	téléphone (m)	[telefɔn]

15. Professions. Social status

director	directeur (m)	[dirɛktœr]
superior	supérieur (m)	[syperjœr]
president	président (m)	[prezidɑ̃]
assistant	assistant (m)	[asistɑ̃]
secretary	secrétaire (m, f)	[səkretɛr]
owner, proprietor	propriétaire (m)	[prɔprijetɛr]
partner	partenaire (m)	[partənɛr]
stockholder	actionnaire (m)	[aksjɔnɛr]
businessman	homme (m) d'affaires	[ɔm dafɛr]
millionaire	millionnaire (m)	[miljɔnɛr]
billionaire	milliardaire (m)	[miljardɛr]
actor	acteur (m)	[aktœr]
architect	architecte (m)	[arʃitɛkt]
banker	banquier (m)	[bɑ̃kje]
broker	courtier (m)	[kurtje]
veterinarian	vétérinaire (m)	[veterinɛr]
doctor	médecin (m)	[medsɛ̃]

chambermaid	femme (f) de chambre	[fam də ʃãbr]
designer	designer (m)	[dizajnœr]
correspondent	correspondant (m)	[kɔrɛspõdã]
delivery man	livreur (m)	[livrœr]

electrician	électricien (m)	[elɛktrisjɛ̃]
musician	musicien (m)	[myzisjɛ̃]
babysitter	baby-sitter (m, f)	[bebisitœr]
hairdresser	coiffeur (m)	[kwafœr]
herder, shepherd	berger (m)	[bɛrʒe]

singer (masc.)	chanteur (m)	[ʃãtœr]
translator	traducteur (m)	[tradyktœr]
writer	écrivain (m)	[ekrivɛ̃]
carpenter	charpentier (m)	[ʃarpãtje]
cook	cuisinier (m)	[kɥizinje]

fireman	pompier (m)	[põpje]
police officer	policier (m)	[pɔlisje]
mailman	facteur (m)	[faktœr]
programmer	programmeur (m)	[prɔgramœr]
salesman (store staff)	vendeur (m)	[vãdœr]

worker	ouvrier (m)	[uvrije]
gardener	jardinier (m)	[ʒardinje]
plumber	plombier (m)	[plõbje]
dentist	stomatologue (m)	[stɔmatɔlɔg]
flight attendant (fem.)	hôtesse (f) de l'air	[otɛs də lɛr]

dancer (masc.)	danseur (m)	[dãsœr]
bodyguard	garde (m) du corps	[gard dy kɔr]
scientist	savant (m)	[savã]
schoolteacher	professeur (m)	[prɔfɛsœr]

farmer	fermier (m)	[fɛrmje]
surgeon	chirurgien (m)	[ʃiryrʒjɛ̃]
miner	mineur (m)	[minœr]
chef (kitchen chef)	cuisinier (m) en chef	[kɥizinje ã ʃɛf]
driver	chauffeur (m)	[ʃofœr]

16. Sport

kind of sports	type (m) de sport	[tip də spɔr]
soccer	football (m)	[futbol]
hockey	hockey (m)	[ɔkɛ]
basketball	basket-ball (m)	[baskɛtbol]
baseball	base-ball (m)	[bɛzbol]

| volleyball | volley-ball (m) | [vɔlɛbol] |
| boxing | boxe (f) | [bɔks] |

wrestling	**lutte** (f)	[lyt]
tennis	**tennis** (m)	[tenis]
swimming	**natation** (f)	[natasjɔ̃]
chess	**échecs** (m pl)	[eʃɛk]
running	**course** (f)	[kurs]
athletics	**athlétisme** (m)	[atletism]
figure skating	**patinage** (m) **artistique**	[patinaʒ artistik]
cycling	**cyclisme** (m)	[siklism]
billiards	**billard** (m)	[bijar]
bodybuilding	**bodybuilding** (m)	[bodibildiŋ]
golf	**golf** (m)	[gɔlf]
scuba diving	**plongée** (f)	[plɔ̃ʒe]
sailing	**voile** (f)	[vwal]
archery	**tir** (m) **à l'arc**	[tir ɑ lark]
period, half	**mi-temps** (f)	[mitɑ̃]
half-time	**mi-temps** (f)	[mitɑ̃]
tie	**match** (m) **nul**	[matʃ nyl]
to tie (vi)	**faire match nul**	[fɛr matʃ nyl]
treadmill	**tapis** (m) **roulant**	[tapi rulɑ̃]
player	**joueur** (m)	[ʒwœr]
substitute	**remplaçant** (m)	[rɑ̃plasɑ̃]
substitutes bench	**banc** (m) **des remplaçants**	[bɑ̃ de rɑ̃plasɑ̃]
match	**match** (m)	[matʃ]
goal	**but** (m)	[byt]
goalkeeper	**gardien** (m) **de but**	[gardjɛ̃ də byt]
goal (score)	**but** (m)	[byt]
Olympic Games	**Jeux** (m pl) **olympiques**	[ʒø zɔlɛ̃pik]
to set a record	**établir un record**	[etablir œ̃ rəkɔr]
final	**finale** (f)	[final]
champion	**champion** (m)	[ʃɑ̃pjɔ̃]
championship	**championnat** (m)	[ʃɑ̃pjɔna]
winner	**gagnant** (m)	[gaɲɑ̃]
victory	**victoire** (f)	[viktwar]
to win (vi)	**gagner** (vi)	[gaɲe]
to lose (not win)	**perdre** (vi)	[pɛrdr]
medal	**médaille** (f)	[medaj]
first place	**première place** (f)	[prəmjɛr plas]
second place	**deuxième place** (f)	[døzjɛm plas]
third place	**troisième place** (f)	[trwazjɛm plas]
stadium	**stade** (m)	[stad]
fan, supporter	**supporteur** (m)	[sypɔrtœr]
trainer, coach	**entraîneur** (m)	[ɑ̃trɛnœr]
training	**entraînement** (m)	[ɑ̃trɛnmɑ̃]

17. Foreign languages. Orthography

language	langue (f)	[lɑ̃g]
to study (vt)	étudier (vt)	[etydje]
pronunciation	prononciation (f)	[prɔnɔ̃sjasjɔ̃]
accent	accent (m)	[aksɑ̃]

noun	nom (m)	[nɔ̃]
adjective	adjectif (m)	[adʒɛktif]
verb	verbe (m)	[vɛrb]
adverb	adverbe (m)	[advɛrb]

pronoun	pronom (m)	[prɔnɔ̃]
interjection	interjection (f)	[ɛ̃tɛrʒɛksjɔ̃]
preposition	préposition (f)	[prepozisjɔ̃]

root	racine (f)	[rasin]
ending	terminaison (f)	[tɛrminɛzɔ̃]
prefix	préfixe (m)	[prefiks]
syllable	syllabe (f)	[silab]
suffix	suffixe (m)	[syfiks]

stress mark	accent (m) tonique	[aksɑ̃ tɔnik]
period, dot	point (m)	[pwɛ̃]
comma	virgule (f)	[virgyl]
colon	deux-points (m)	[døpwɛ̃]
ellipsis	points (m pl) de suspension	[pwɛ̃ də syspɑ̃sjɔ̃]

question	question (f)	[kɛstjɔ̃]
question mark	point (m) d'interrogation	[pwɛ̃ dɛ̃terɔgasjɔ̃]
exclamation point	point (m) d'exclamation	[pwɛ̃ dɛksklamasjɔ̃]

in quotation marks	entre guillemets	[ɑ̃tr gijmɛ]
in parenthesis	entre parenthèses	[ɑ̃tr parɑ̃tɛz]
letter	lettre (f)	[lɛtr]
capital letter	majuscule (f)	[maʒyskyl]

sentence	proposition (f)	[prɔpozisjɔ̃]
group of words	groupe (m) de mots	[grup də mo]
expression	expression (f)	[ɛkspresjɔ̃]

subject	sujet (m)	[syʒɛ]
predicate	prédicat (m)	[predika]
line	ligne (f)	[liɲ]
paragraph	paragraphe (m)	[paragraf]

synonym	synonyme (m)	[sinɔnim]
antonym	antonyme (m)	[ɑ̃tɔnim]
exception	exception (f)	[ɛksɛpsjɔ̃]
to underline (vt)	souligner (vt)	[suliɲe]

rules	**règles** (f pl)	[rɛgl]
grammar	**grammaire** (f)	[gramɛr]
vocabulary	**vocabulaire** (m)	[vɔkabylɛr]
phonetics	**phonétique** (f)	[fɔnetik]
alphabet	**alphabet** (m)	[alfabɛ]

textbook	**manuel** (m)	[manɥɛl]
dictionary	**dictionnaire** (m)	[diksjɔnɛr]
phrasebook	**guide** (m) **de conversation**	[gid də kɔ̃vɛrsasjɔ̃]

word	**mot** (m)	[mo]
meaning	**sens** (m)	[sɑ̃s]
memory	**mémoire** (f)	[memwar]

18. The Earth. Geography

the Earth	**Terre** (f)	[tɛr]
the globe (the Earth)	**globe** (m) **terrestre**	[glɔb tɛrɛstr]
planet	**planète** (f)	[planɛt]

geography	**géographie** (f)	[ʒeɔgrafi]
nature	**nature** (f)	[natyr]
map	**carte** (f)	[kart]
atlas	**atlas** (m)	[atlas]

in the north	**au nord**	[onɔr]
in the south	**au sud**	[osyd]
in the west	**à l'occident**	[alɔksidɑ̃]
in the east	**à l'orient**	[alɔrjɑ̃]

sea	**mer** (f)	[mɛr]
ocean	**océan** (m)	[ɔseɑ̃]
gulf (bay)	**golfe** (m)	[gɔlf]
straits	**détroit** (m)	[detrwa]

continent (mainland)	**continent** (m)	[kɔ̃tinɑ̃]
island	**île** (f)	[il]
peninsula	**presqu'île** (f)	[prɛskil]
archipelago	**archipel** (m)	[arʃipɛl]

harbor	**port** (m)	[pɔr]
coral reef	**récif** (m) **de corail**	[resif də kɔraj]
shore	**littoral** (m)	[litɔral]
coast	**côte** (f)	[kot]

flow (flood tide)	**marée** (f) **haute**	[mare ot]
ebb (ebb tide)	**marée** (f) **basse**	[mare bas]
latitude	**latitude** (f)	[latityd]
longitude	**longitude** (f)	[lɔ̃ʒityd]

parallel	parallèle (f)	[paralɛl]
equator	équateur (m)	[ekwatœr]
sky	ciel (m)	[sjɛl]
horizon	horizon (m)	[ɔrizɔ̃]
atmosphere	atmosphère (f)	[atmɔsfɛr]
mountain	montagne (f)	[mɔ̃taɲ]
summit, top	sommet (m)	[sɔmɛ]
cliff	rocher (m)	[rɔʃe]
hill	colline (f)	[kɔlin]
volcano	volcan (m)	[vɔlkã]
glacier	glacier (m)	[glasje]
waterfall	chute (f) d'eau	[ʃyt do]
plain	plaine (f)	[plɛn]
river	rivière (f), fleuve (m)	[rivjɛr], [flœv]
spring (natural source)	source (f)	[surs]
bank (of river)	rive (f)	[riv]
downstream (adv)	en aval	[ɑn aval]
upstream (adv)	en amont	[ɑn amɔ̃]
lake	lac (m)	[lak]
dam	barrage (m)	[baraʒ]
canal	canal (m)	[kanal]
swamp (marshland)	marais (m)	[marɛ]
ice	glace (f)	[glas]

19. Countries of the world. Part 1

Europe	Europe (f)	[ørɔp]
European Union	Union (f) européenne	[ynjɔn ørɔpeɛn]
European (n)	européen (m)	[ørɔpeɛ̃]
European (adj)	européen (adj)	[ørɔpeɛ̃]
Austria	Autriche (f)	[otriʃ]
Great Britain	Grande-Bretagne (f)	[grɑ̃dbrətaɲ]
England	Angleterre (f)	[ɑ̃glətɛr]
Belgium	Belgique (f)	[bɛlʒik]
Germany	Allemagne (f)	[almaɲ]
Netherlands	Pays-Bas (m)	[peiba]
Holland	Hollande (f)	[ɔlɑ̃d]
Greece	Grèce (f)	[grɛs]
Denmark	Danemark (m)	[danmark]
Ireland	Irlande (f)	[irlɑ̃d]
Iceland	Islande (f)	[islɑ̃d]
Spain	Espagne (f)	[ɛspaɲ]

Italy	Italie (f)	[itali]
Cyprus	Chypre (m)	[ʃipr]
Malta	Malte (f)	[malt]

Norway	Norvège (f)	[nɔrvɛʒ]
Portugal	Portugal (m)	[pɔrtygal]
Finland	Finlande (f)	[fɛ̃lɑ̃d]
France	France (f)	[frɑ̃s]
Sweden	Suède (f)	[sɥɛd]

Switzerland	Suisse (f)	[sɥis]
Scotland	Écosse (f)	[ekɔs]
Vatican	Vatican (m)	[vatikɑ̃]
Liechtenstein	Liechtenstein (m)	[liʃtɛnʃtajn]
Luxembourg	Luxembourg (m)	[lyksɑ̃bur]

Monaco	Monaco (m)	[mɔnako]
Albania	Albanie (f)	[albani]
Bulgaria	Bulgarie (f)	[bylgari]
Hungary	Hongrie (f)	[ɔ̃gri]
Latvia	Lettonie (f)	[lɛtɔni]

Lithuania	Lituanie (f)	[litɥani]
Poland	Pologne (f)	[pɔlɔɲ]
Romania	Roumanie (f)	[rumani]
Serbia	Serbie (f)	[sɛrbi]
Slovakia	Slovaquie (f)	[slɔvaki]

Croatia	Croatie (f)	[krɔasi]
Czech Republic	République (f) Tchèque	[repyblik tʃɛk]
Estonia	Estonie (f)	[ɛstɔni]
Bosnia and Herzegovina	Bosnie (f)	[bɔsni]
Macedonia (Republic of ~)	Macédoine (f)	[masedwan]

Slovenia	Slovénie (f)	[slɔveni]
Montenegro	Monténégro (m)	[mɔ̃tenegro]
Belarus	Biélorussie (f)	[bjelɔrysi]
Moldova, Moldavia	Moldavie (f)	[mɔldavi]
Russia	Russie (f)	[rysi]
Ukraine	Ukraine (f)	[ykrɛn]

20. Countries of the world. Part 2

Asia	Asie (f)	[azi]
Vietnam	Vietnam (m)	[vjɛtnam]
India	Inde (f)	[ɛ̃d]
Israel	Israël (m)	[israɛl]
China	Chine (f)	[ʃin]
Lebanon	Liban (m)	[libɑ̃]
Mongolia	Mongolie (f)	[mɔ̃gɔli]

Malaysia	Malaisie (f)	[malɛzi]
Pakistan	Pakistan (m)	[pakistɑ̃]
Saudi Arabia	Arabie (f) Saoudite	[arabi saudit]
Thailand	Thaïlande (f)	[tajlɑ̃d]
Taiwan	Taïwan (m)	[tajwan]
Turkey	Turquie (f)	[tyrki]
Japan	Japon (m)	[ʒapɔ̃]
Afghanistan	Afghanistan (m)	[afganistɑ̃]
Bangladesh	Bangladesh (m)	[bɑ̃gladɛʃ]
Indonesia	Indonésie (f)	[ɛ̃dɔnezi]
Jordan	Jordanie (f)	[ʒɔrdani]
Iraq	Iraq (m)	[irak]
Iran	Iran (m)	[irɑ̃]
Cambodia	Cambodge (m)	[kɑ̃bɔdʒ]
Kuwait	Koweït (m)	[kɔwɛjt]
Laos	Laos (m)	[laos]
Myanmar	Myanmar (m)	[mjanmar]
Nepal	Népal (m)	[nepal]
United Arab Emirates	Fédération (f) des Émirats Arabes Unis	[federasjɔ̃ dezemira arabzyni]
Syria	Syrie (f)	[siri]
Palestine	Palestine (f)	[palɛstin]
South Korea	Corée (f) du Sud	[kɔre dy syd]
North Korea	Corée (f) du Nord	[kɔre dy nɔr]
United States of America	les États Unis	[lezeta zyni]
Canada	Canada (m)	[kanada]
Mexico	Mexique (m)	[mɛksik]
Argentina	Argentine (f)	[arʒɑ̃tin]
Brazil	Brésil (m)	[brezil]
Colombia	Colombie (f)	[kɔlɔ̃bi]
Cuba	Cuba (f)	[kyba]
Chile	Chili (m)	[ʃili]
Venezuela	Venezuela (f)	[venezɥela]
Ecuador	Équateur (m)	[ekwatœr]
The Bahamas	Bahamas (f pl)	[baamas]
Panama	Panamá (m)	[panama]
Egypt	Égypte (f)	[eʒipt]
Morocco	Maroc (m)	[marɔk]
Tunisia	Tunisie (f)	[tynizi]
Kenya	Kenya (m)	[kenja]
Libya	Libye (f)	[libi]
South Africa	République (f) Sud-africaine	[repyblik sydafrikɛn]
Australia	Australie (f)	[ostrali]
New Zealand	Nouvelle Zélande (f)	[nuvɛl zelɑ̃d]

21. Weather. Natural disasters

weather	**temps** (m)	[tã]
weather forecast	**météo** (f)	[meteo]
temperature	**température** (f)	[tãperatyr]
thermometer	**thermomètre** (m)	[tɛrmɔmɛtr]
barometer	**baromètre** (m)	[barɔmɛtr]
sun	**soleil** (m)	[sɔlɛj]
to shine (vi)	**briller** (vi)	[brije]
sunny (day)	**ensoleillé** (adj)	[ãsɔleje]
to come up (vi)	**se lever** (vp)	[sə ləve]
to set (vi)	**se coucher** (vp)	[sə kuʃe]
rain	**pluie** (f)	[plɥi]
it's raining	**il pleut**	[il plø]
pouring rain	**pluie** (f) **torrentielle**	[plɥi tɔrãsjɛl]
rain cloud	**nuée** (f)	[nɥe]
puddle	**flaque** (f)	[flak]
to get wet (in rain)	**se faire mouiller**	[sə fɛr muje]
thunderstorm	**orage** (m)	[ɔraʒ]
lightning (~ strike)	**éclair** (m)	[eklɛr]
to flash (vi)	**éclater** (vi)	[eklate]
thunder	**tonnerre** (m)	[tɔnɛr]
it's thundering	**le tonnerre gronde**	[lə tɔnɛr grõd]
hail	**grêle** (f)	[grɛl]
it's hailing	**il grêle**	[il grɛl]
heat (extreme ~)	**chaleur** (f)	[ʃalœr]
it's hot	**il fait très chaud**	[il fɛ trɛ ʃo]
it's warm	**il fait chaud**	[il fɛʃo]
it's cold	**il fait froid**	[il fɛ frwa]
fog (mist)	**brouillard** (m)	[brujar]
foggy	**brumeux** (adj)	[brymø]
cloud	**nuage** (m)	[nɥaʒ]
cloudy (adj)	**nuageux** (adj)	[nɥaʒø]
humidity	**humidité** (f)	[ymidite]
snow	**neige** (f)	[nɛʒ]
it's snowing	**il neige**	[il nɛʒ]
frost (severe ~, freezing cold)	**gel** (m)	[ʒɛl]
below zero (adv)	**au-dessous de zéro**	[odsu də zero]
hoarfrost	**givre** (m)	[ʒivr]
bad weather	**intempéries** (f pl)	[ɛ̃tãperi]
disaster	**catastrophe** (f)	[katastrɔf]
flood, inundation	**inondation** (f)	[inõdasjõ]
avalanche	**avalanche** (f)	[avalãʃ]

earthquake	tremblement (m) de terre	[trăbləmă də tɛr]
tremor, quake	secousse (f)	[səkus]
epicenter	épicentre (m)	[episɑ̃tr]
eruption	éruption (f)	[erypsjɔ̃]
lava	lave (f)	[lav]

tornado	tornade (f)	[tɔrnad]
twister	tourbillon (m)	[turbijɔ̃]
hurricane	ouragan (m)	[uragɑ̃]
tsunami	tsunami (m)	[tsynami]
cyclone	cyclone (m)	[siklon]

22. Animals. Part 1

| animal | animal (m) | [animal] |
| predator | prédateur (m) | [predatœr] |

tiger	tigre (m)	[tigr]
lion	lion (m)	[ljɔ̃]
wolf	loup (m)	[lu]
fox	renard (m)	[rənar]
jaguar	jaguar (m)	[ʒagwar]

lynx	lynx (m)	[lɛ̃ks]
coyote	coyote (m)	[kɔjɔt]
jackal	chacal (m)	[ʃakal]
hyena	hyène (f)	[jɛn]

squirrel	écureuil (m)	[ekyrœj]
hedgehog	hérisson (m)	[erisɔ̃]
rabbit	lapin (m)	[lapɛ̃]
raccoon	raton (m)	[ratɔ̃]

hamster	hamster (m)	[amstɛr]
mole	taupe (f)	[top]
mouse	souris (f)	[suri]
rat	rat (m)	[ra]
bat	chauve-souris (f)	[ʃovsuri]

beaver	castor (m)	[kastɔr]
horse	cheval (m)	[ʃəval]
deer	cerf (m)	[sɛr]
camel	chameau (m)	[ʃamo]
zebra	zèbre (m)	[zɛbr]

whale	baleine (f)	[balɛn]
seal	phoque (m)	[fɔk]
walrus	morse (m)	[mɔrs]
dolphin	dauphin (m)	[dofɛ̃]
bear	ours (m)	[urs]

monkey	singe (m)	[sɛ̃ʒ]
elephant	éléphant (m)	[elefɑ̃]
rhinoceros	rhinocéros (m)	[rinɔserɔs]
giraffe	girafe (f)	[ʒiraf]
hippopotamus	hippopotame (m)	[ipɔpɔtam]
kangaroo	kangourou (m)	[kɑ̃guru]
cat	chat (m)	[ʃa]
dog	chien (m)	[ʃjɛ̃]
cow	vache (f)	[vaʃ]
bull	taureau (m)	[tɔro]
sheep (ewe)	brebis (f)	[brɛbi]
goat	chèvre (f)	[ʃɛvr]
donkey	âne (m)	[ɑn]
pig, hog	cochon (m)	[kɔʃɔ̃]
hen (chicken)	poule (f)	[pul]
rooster	coq (m)	[kɔk]
duck	canard (m)	[kanar]
goose	oie (f)	[wa]
turkey (hen)	dinde (f)	[dɛ̃d]
sheepdog	berger (m)	[bɛrʒe]

23. Animals. Part 2

bird	oiseau (m)	[wazo]
pigeon	pigeon (m)	[piʒɔ̃]
sparrow	moineau (m)	[mwano]
tit	mésange (f)	[mezɑ̃ʒ]
magpie	pie (f)	[pi]
eagle	aigle (m)	[ɛgl]
hawk	épervier (m)	[epɛrvje]
falcon	faucon (m)	[fokɔ̃]
swan	cygne (m)	[siɲ]
crane	grue (f)	[gry]
stork	cigogne (f)	[sigɔɲ]
parrot	perroquet (m)	[perɔkɛ]
peacock	paon (m)	[pɑ̃]
ostrich	autruche (f)	[otryʃ]
heron	héron (m)	[erɔ̃]
nightingale	rossignol (m)	[rɔsiɲɔl]
swallow	hirondelle (f)	[irɔ̃dɛl]
woodpecker	pivert (m)	[pivɛr]
cuckoo	coucou (m)	[kuku]
owl	chouette (f)	[ʃwɛt]

penguin	pingouin (m)	[pɛ̃gwɛ̃]
tuna	thon (m)	[tɔ̃]
trout	truite (f)	[trɥit]
eel	anguille (f)	[ãgij]

shark	requin (m)	[rəkɛ̃]
crab	crabe (m)	[krab]
jellyfish	méduse (f)	[medyz]
octopus	pieuvre (f), poulpe (m)	[pjœvr], [pulp]

starfish	étoile (f) de mer	[etwal də mɛr]
sea urchin	oursin (m)	[ursɛ̃]
seahorse	hippocampe (m)	[ipɔkãp]
shrimp	crevette (f)	[krəvɛt]

snake	serpent (m)	[sɛrpã]
viper	vipère (f)	[vipɛr]
lizard	lézard (m)	[lezar]
iguana	iguane (m)	[igwan]
chameleon	caméléon (m)	[kameleɔ̃]
scorpion	scorpion (m)	[skɔrpjɔ̃]

turtle	tortue (f)	[tɔrty]
frog	grenouille (f)	[grənuj]
crocodile	crocodile (m)	[krɔkɔdil]

insect, bug	insecte (m)	[ɛ̃sɛkt]
butterfly	papillon (m)	[papijɔ̃]
ant	fourmi (f)	[furmi]
fly	mouche (f)	[muʃ]

mosquito	moustique (m)	[mustik]
beetle	scarabée (m)	[skarabe]
bee	abeille (f)	[abɛj]
spider	araignée (f)	[arɛɲe]

24. Trees. Plants

tree	arbre (m)	[arbr]
birch	bouleau (m)	[bulo]
oak	chêne (m)	[ʃɛn]
linden tree	tilleul (m)	[tijœl]
aspen	tremble (m)	[trãbl]

maple	érable (m)	[erabl]
spruce	épicéa (m)	[episea]
pine	pin (m)	[pɛ̃]
cedar	cèdre (m)	[sɛdr]
poplar	peuplier (m)	[pøplije]
rowan	sorbier (m)	[sɔrbje]

| beech | hêtre (m) | [ɛtr] |
| elm | orme (m) | [ɔrm] |

ash (tree)	frêne (m)	[frɛn]
chestnut	marronnier (m)	[marɔnje]
palm tree	palmier (m)	[palmje]
bush	buisson (m)	[bɥisɔ̃]

mushroom	champignon (m)	[ʃɑ̃piɲɔ̃]
poisonous mushroom	champignon (m) vénéneux	[ʃɑ̃piɲɔ̃ venenø]
cep (Boletus edulis)	cèpe (m)	[sɛp]
russula	russule (f)	[rysyl]
fly agaric	amanite (f) tue-mouches	[amanit tymuʃ]
death cap	oronge (f) verte	[ɔrɔ̃ʒ vɛrt]

flower	fleur (f)	[flœr]
bouquet (of flowers)	bouquet (m)	[bukɛ]
rose (flower)	rose (f)	[roz]

| tulip | tulipe (f) | [tylip] |
| carnation | oeillet (m) | [œjɛ] |

camomile	marguerite (f)	[margərit]
cactus	cactus (m)	[kaktys]
lily of the valley	muguet (m)	[mygɛ]

| snowdrop | perce-neige (f) | [pɛrsənɛʒ] |
| water lily | nénuphar (m) | [nenyfar] |

greenhouse (tropical ~)	serre (f) tropicale	[sɛr trɔpikal]
lawn	gazon (m)	[gazɔ̃]
flowerbed	parterre (m) de fleurs	[partɛr də flœr]

plant	plante (f)	[plɑ̃t]
grass	herbe (f)	[ɛrb]
leaf	feuille (f)	[fœj]
petal	pétale (m)	[petal]

| stem | tige (f) | [tiʒ] |
| young plant (shoot) | pousse (f) | [pus] |

| cereal crops | céréales (f pl) | [sereal] |
| wheat | blé (m) | [ble] |

| rye | seigle (m) | [sɛgl] |
| oats | avoine (f) | [avwan] |

millet	millet (m)	[mijɛ]
barley	orge (f)	[ɔrʒ]
corn	maïs (m)	[mais]
rice	riz (m)	[ri]

25. Various useful words

balance (of situation)	**balance** (f)	[balɑ̃s]
base (basis)	**base** (f)	[baz]
beginning	**début** (m)	[debu]
category	**catégorie** (f)	[kategɔri]
choice	**choix** (m)	[ʃwa]
coincidence	**coïncidence** (f)	[kɔɛ̃sidɑ̃s]
comparison	**comparaison** (f)	[kɔ̃parɛzɔ̃]
degree (extent, amount)	**degré** (m)	[dəgre]
development	**développement** (m)	[devlɔpmɑ̃]
difference	**différence** (f)	[diferɑ̃s]
effect (e.g., of drugs)	**effet** (m)	[efɛ]
effort (exertion)	**effort** (m)	[efɔr]
element	**élément** (m)	[elemɑ̃]
example (illustration)	**exemple** (m)	[ɛgzɑ̃p]
fact	**fait** (m)	[fɛ]
help	**aide** (f)	[ɛd]
ideal	**idéal** (m)	[ideal]
kind (sort, type)	**type** (m)	[tip]
mistake, error	**faute** (f)	[fot]
moment	**moment** (m)	[mɔmɑ̃]
obstacle	**obstacle** (m)	[ɔpstakl]
part (~ of sth)	**part** (f)	[par]
pause (break)	**pause** (f)	[poz]
position	**position** (f)	[pozisjɔ̃]
problem	**problème** (m)	[prɔblɛm]
process	**processus** (m)	[prɔsesys]
progress	**progrès** (m)	[prɔgrɛ]
property (quality)	**propriété** (f)	[prɔprijete]
reaction	**réaction** (f)	[reaksjɔ̃]
risk	**risque** (m)	[risk]
secret	**secret** (m)	[səkrɛ]
series	**série** (f)	[seri]
shape (outer form)	**forme** (f)	[fɔrm]
situation	**situation** (f)	[situasjɔ̃]
solution	**solution** (f)	[sɔlysjɔ̃]
standard (adj)	**standard** (adj)	[stɑ̃dar]
stop (pause)	**arrêt** (m)	[arɛ]
style	**style** (m)	[stil]
system	**système** (m)	[sistɛm]

table (chart)	**tableau** (m)	[tablo]
tempo, rate	**tempo** (m)	[tɛmpo]
term (word, expression)	**terme** (m)	[tɛrm]
truth (e.g., moment of ~)	**vérité** (f)	[verite]
turn (please wait your ~)	**tour** (m)	[tur]
urgent (adj)	**urgent** (adj)	[yrʒɑ̃]
utility (usefulness)	**utilité** (f)	[ytilite]
variant (alternative)	**version** (f)	[vɛrsjɔ̃]
way (means, method)	**mode** (m)	[mɔd]
zone	**zone** (f)	[zon]

26. Modifiers. Adjectives. Part 1

additional (adj)	**supplémentaire** (adj)	[syplemɑ̃tɛr]
ancient (~ civilization)	**ancien** (adj)	[ɑ̃sjɛ̃]
artificial (adj)	**artificiel** (adj)	[artifisjɛl]
bad (adj)	**mauvais** (adj)	[movɛ]
beautiful (person)	**beau** (adj)	[bo]
big (in size)	**grand** (adj)	[grɑ̃]
bitter (taste)	**amer** (adj)	[amɛr]
blind (sightless)	**aveugle** (adj)	[avœgl]
central (adj)	**central** (adj)	[sɑ̃tral]
children's (adj)	**d'enfant** (adj)	[dɑ̃fɑ̃]
clandestine (secret)	**clandestin** (adj)	[klɑ̃dɛstɛ̃]
clean (free from dirt)	**propre** (adj)	[prɔpr]
clever (smart)	**intelligent** (adj)	[ɛ̃teliʒɑ̃]
compatible (adj)	**compatible** (adj)	[kɔ̃patibl]
contented (satisfied)	**content** (adj)	[kɔ̃tɑ̃]
dangerous (adj)	**dangereux** (adj)	[dɑ̃ʒrø]
dead (not alive)	**mort** (adj)	[mɔr]
dense (fog, smoke)	**dense** (adj)	[dɑ̃s]
difficult (decision)	**difficile** (adj)	[difisil]
dirty (not clean)	**sale** (adj)	[sal]
easy (not difficult)	**facile** (adj)	[fasil]
empty (glass, room)	**vide** (adj)	[vid]
exact (amount)	**précis, exact** (adj)	[presi], [ɛgzakt]
excellent (adj)	**excellent** (adj)	[ɛksɛlɑ̃]
excessive (adj)	**excessif** (adj)	[ɛksesif]
exterior (adj)	**extérieur** (adj)	[ɛksterjœr]
fast (quick)	**rapide** (adj)	[rapid]
fertile (land, soil)	**fertile** (adj)	[fɛrtil]
fragile (china, glass)	**fragile** (adj)	[fraʒil]
free (at no cost)	**gratuit** (adj)	[gratɥi]

fresh (~ water)	douce (adj)	[dus]
frozen (food)	surgelé (adj)	[syrʒele]
full (completely filled)	plein (adj)	[plɛ̃]
happy (adj)	heureux (adj)	[œrø]
hard (not soft)	dur (adj)	[dyr]
huge (adj)	géant (adj)	[ʒeɑ̃]
ill (sick, unwell)	malade (adj)	[malad]
immobile (adj)	immobile (adj)	[imɔbil]
important (adj)	important (adj)	[ɛ̃pɔrtɑ̃]
interior (adj)	intérieur (adj)	[ɛ̃terjœr]
last (e.g., ~ week)	passé (adj)	[pɑse]
last (final)	dernier (adj)	[dɛrnje]
left (e.g., ~ side)	gauche (adj)	[goʃ]
legal (legitimate)	légal (adj)	[legal]
light (in weight)	léger (adj)	[leʒe]
liquid (fluid)	liquide (adj)	[likid]
long (e.g., ~ hair)	long (adj)	[lɔ̃]
loud (voice, etc.)	fort (adj)	[fɔr]
low (voice)	bas (adj)	[ba]

27. Modifiers. Adjectives. Part 2

main (principal)	principal (adj)	[prɛ̃sipal]
matt, matte	mat (adj)	[mat]
mysterious (adj)	mystérieux (adj)	[misterjø]
narrow (street, etc.)	étroit (adj)	[etrwa]
native (~ country)	natal (adj)	[natal]
negative (~ response)	négatif (adj)	[negatif]
new (adj)	neuf (adj)	[nœf]
next (e.g., ~ week)	suivant (adj)	[sɥivɑ̃]
normal (adj)	normal (adj)	[nɔrmal]
not difficult (adj)	facile (adj)	[fasil]
obligatory (adj)	obligatoire (adj)	[ɔbligatwar]
old (house)	vieux (adj)	[vjø]
open (adj)	ouvert (adj)	[uvɛr]
opposite (adj)	opposé (adj)	[ɔpoze]
ordinary (usual)	ordinaire (adj)	[ɔrdinɛr]
original (unusual)	original (adj)	[ɔriʒinal]
personal (adj)	personnel (adj)	[pɛrsɔnɛl]
polite (adj)	poli (adj)	[pɔli]
poor (not rich)	pauvre (adj)	[povr]
possible (adj)	possible (adj)	[pɔsibl]
principal (main)	principal (adj)	[prɛ̃sipal]

probable (adj)	probable (adj)	[prɔbabl]
prolonged (e.g., ~ applause)	continu (adj)	[kɔ̃tiny]
public (open to all)	public (adj)	[pyblik]
rare (adj)	rare (adj)	[rar]
raw (uncooked)	cru (adj)	[kry]
right (not left)	droit (adj)	[drwa]
ripe (fruit)	mûr (adj)	[myr]
risky (adj)	risqué (adj)	[riske]
sad (~ look)	triste (adj)	[trist]
second hand (adj)	d'occasion (adj)	[dɔkazjɔ̃]
shallow (water)	peu profond (adj)	[pø prɔfɔ̃]
sharp (blade, etc.)	bien affilé (adj)	[bjɛn afile]
short (in length)	court (adj)	[kur]
similar (adj)	similaire, pareil (adj)	[similɛr], [parɛj]
small (in size)	petit (adj)	[pti]
smooth (surface)	lisse (adj)	[lis]
soft (~ toys)	mou (adj)	[mu]
solid (~ wall)	solide (adj)	[sɔlid]
sour (flavor, taste)	aigre (adj)	[ɛgr]
spacious (house, etc.)	spacieux (adj)	[spasjø]
special (adj)	spécial (adj)	[spesjal]
straight (line, road)	droit (adj)	[drwa]
strong (person)	fort (adj)	[fɔr]
stupid (foolish)	stupide (adj)	[stypid]
superb, perfect (adj)	parfait (adj)	[parfɛ]
sweet (sugary)	sucré (adj)	[sykre]
tan (adj)	bronzé (adj)	[brɔ̃ze]
tasty (delicious)	bon, savoureux (adj)	[bɔ̃], [savurø]
unclear (adj)	pas clair (adj)	[pɑ klɛr]

28. Verbs. Part 1

to accuse (vt)	accuser (vt)	[akyze]
to agree (say yes)	être d'accord	[ɛtr dakɔr]
to announce (vt)	annoncer (vt)	[anɔ̃se]
to answer (vi, vt)	répondre (vi, vt)	[repɔ̃dr]
to apologize (vi)	s'excuser (vp)	[sɛkskyze]
to arrive (vi)	venir (vi)	[vənir]
to ask (~ oneself)	demander (vt)	[dəmɑ̃de]
to be absent	être absent	[ɛtr apsɑ̃]
to be afraid	avoir peur	[avwar pœr]
to be born	naître (vi)	[nɛtr]

to be in a hurry	se dépêcher	[sə depeʃe]
to beat (to hit)	battre (vt)	[batr]
to begin (vt)	commencer (vt)	[kɔmɑ̃se]
to believe (in God)	croire (vi)	[krwar]
to belong to ...	appartenir à ...	[apartənir a]
to break (split into pieces)	casser (vt)	[kase]
to build (vt)	construire (vt)	[kɔ̃strɥir]
to buy (purchase)	acheter (vt)	[aʃte]
can (v aux)	pouvoir (v aux)	[puvwar]
can (v aux)	pouvoir (v aux)	[puvwar]
to cancel (call off)	annuler (vt)	[anyle]
to catch (vt)	attraper (vt)	[atrape]
to change (vt)	changer (vt)	[ʃɑ̃ʒe]
to check (to examine)	vérifier (vt)	[verifje]
to choose (select)	choisir (vt)	[ʃwazir]
to clean up (tidy)	faire le ménage	[fɛr le menaʒ]
to close (vt)	fermer (vt)	[fɛrme]
to compare (vt)	comparer (vt)	[kɔ̃pare]
to complain (vi, vt)	se plaindre (vp)	[sə plɛ̃dr]
to confirm (vt)	confirmer (vt)	[kɔ̃firme]
to congratulate (vt)	féliciter (vt)	[felisite]
to cook (dinner)	préparer (vt)	[prepare]
to copy (vt)	copier (vt)	[kɔpje]
to cost (vt)	coûter (vt)	[kute]
to count (add up)	compter (vi, vt)	[kɔ̃te]
to count on ...	compter sur ...	[kɔ̃te syr]
to create (vt)	créer (vt)	[kree]
to cry (weep)	pleurer (vi)	[plœre]
to dance (vi, vt)	danser (vi, vt)	[dɑ̃se]
to deceive (vi, vt)	tromper (vt)	[trɔ̃pe]
to decide (~ to do sth)	décider (vt)	[deside]
to delete (vt)	supprimer (vt)	[syprime]
to demand (request firmly)	exiger (vt)	[ɛgziʒe]
to deny (vt)	nier (vt)	[nje]
to depend on ...	dépendre de ...	[depɑ̃dr də]
to despise (vt)	mépriser (vt)	[meprize]
to die (vi)	mourir (vi)	[murir]
to dig (vt)	creuser (vt)	[krøze]
to disappear (vi)	disparaître (vi)	[disparɛtr]
to discuss (vt)	discuter (vt)	[diskyte]
to disturb (vt)	déranger (vt)	[derɑ̃ʒe]

29. Verbs. Part 2

to dive (vi)	plonger (vi)	[plɔ̃ʒe]
to divorce (vi)	divorcer (vi)	[divɔrse]
to do (vt)	faire (vt)	[fɛr]
to doubt (have doubts)	douter (vt)	[dute]
to drink (vi, vt)	boire (vt)	[bwar]

to drop (let fall)	faire tomber	[fɛr tɔ̃be]
to dry (clothes, hair)	sécher (vt)	[seʃe]
to eat (vi, vt)	manger (vi, vt)	[mɑ̃ʒe]
to end (~ a relationship)	rompre (vt)	[rɔ̃pr]
to excuse (forgive)	excuser (vt)	[ɛkskyze]

to exist (vi)	exister (vi)	[ɛgziste]
to expect (foresee)	prévoir (vt)	[prevwar]
to explain (vt)	expliquer (vt)	[ɛksplike]
to fall (vi)	tomber (vi)	[tɔ̃be]
to fight (street fight, etc.)	se battre (vp)	[sə batr]
to find (vt)	trouver (vt)	[truve]

to finish (vt)	finir (vt)	[finir]
to fly (vi)	voler (vi)	[vɔle]
to forbid (vt)	interdire (vt)	[ɛ̃tɛrdir]
to forget (vi, vt)	oublier (vt)	[ublije]
to forgive (vt)	pardonner (vt)	[pardɔne]

to get tired	être fatigué	[ɛtr fatige]
to give (vt)	donner (vt)	[dɔne]
to go (on foot)	aller (vi)	[ale]
to hate (vt)	haïr (vt)	[air]

to have (vt)	avoir (vt)	[avwar]
to have breakfast	prendre le petit déjeuner	[prɑ̃dr ləpti deʒœne]
to have dinner	dîner (vi)	[dine]
to have lunch	déjeuner (vi)	[deʒœne]

to hear (vt)	entendre (vt)	[ɑ̃tɑ̃dr]
to help (vt)	aider (vt)	[ede]
to hide (vt)	cacher (vt)	[kaʃe]
to hope (vi, vt)	espérer (vi)	[ɛspere]
to hunt (vi, vt)	chasser (vi, vt)	[ʃase]
to hurry (vi)	être pressé	[ɛtr prese]

to insist (vi, vt)	insister (vi)	[ɛ̃siste]
to insult (vt)	insulter (vt)	[ɛ̃sylte]
to invite (vt)	inviter (vt)	[ɛ̃vite]
to joke (vi)	plaisanter (vi)	[plɛzɑ̃te]
to keep (vt)	garder (vt)	[garde]
to kill (vt)	tuer (vt)	[tɥe]
to know (sb)	connaître (vt)	[kɔnɛtr]

to know (sth)	savoir (vt)	[savwar]
to like (I like ...)	plaire (vt)	[plɛr]
to look at ...	regarder (vt)	[rəgarde]

to lose (umbrella, etc.)	perdre (vt)	[pɛrdr]
to love (sb)	aimer (vt)	[eme]
to make a mistake	se tromper (vp)	[sə trɔ̃pe]
to meet (vi, vt)	se rencontrer (vp)	[sə rɑ̃kɔ̃tre]
to miss (school, etc.)	manquer (vt)	[mɑ̃ke]

30. Verbs. Part 3

to obey (vi, vt)	obéir (vt)	[ɔbeir]
to open (vt)	ouvrir (vt)	[uvrir]
to participate (vi)	participer (vi)	[partisipe]
to pay (vi, vt)	payer (vi, vt)	[peje]
to permit (vt)	permettre (vt)	[pɛrmɛtr]

to play (children)	jouer (vt)	[ʒwe]
to pray (vi, vt)	prier (vt)	[prije]
to promise (vt)	promettre (vt)	[prɔmɛtr]
to propose (vt)	proposer (vt)	[prɔpoze]
to prove (vt)	prouver (vt)	[pruve]
to read (vi, vt)	lire (vi, vt)	[lir]

to receive (vt)	recevoir (vt)	[rəsəvwar]
to rent (sth from sb)	louer (vt)	[lwe]
to repeat (say again)	répéter (vt)	[repete]
to reserve, to book	réserver (vt)	[rezɛrve]
to run (vi)	courir (vt)	[kurir]

to save (rescue)	sauver (vt)	[sove]
to say (~ thank you)	dire (vt)	[dir]
to see (vt)	voir (vt)	[vwar]
to sell (vt)	vendre (vt)	[vɑ̃dr]
to send (vt)	envoyer (vt)	[ɑ̃vwaje]
to shoot (vi)	tirer (vi)	[tire]

to shout (vi)	crier (vi)	[krije]
to show (vt)	montrer (vt)	[mɔ̃tre]
to sign (document)	signer (vt)	[siɲe]
to sing (vi)	chanter (vi)	[ʃɑ̃te]
to sit down (vi)	s'asseoir (vp)	[saswar]

to smile (vi)	sourire (vi)	[surir]
to speak (vi, vt)	parler (vi, vt)	[parle]
to steal (money, etc.)	voler (vt)	[vɔle]
to stop (please ~ calling me)	cesser (vt)	[sese]
to study (vt)	étudier (vt)	[etydje]

to swim (vi)	nager (vi)	[naʒe]
to take (vt)	prendre (vt)	[prɑ̃dr]
to talk to ...	parler avec ...	[parle avɛk]
to tell (story, joke)	raconter (vt)	[rakɔ̃te]
to thank (vt)	remercier (vt)	[rəmɛrsje]
to think (vi, vt)	penser (vi, vt)	[pɑ̃se]
to translate (vt)	traduire (vt)	[tradɥir]
to trust (vt)	avoir confiance	[avwar kɔ̃fjɑ̃s]
to try (attempt)	essayer (vt)	[eseje]
to turn (e.g., ~ left)	tourner (vi)	[turne]
to turn off	éteindre (vt)	[etɛ̃dr]
to turn on	allumer (vt)	[alyme]
to understand (vt)	comprendre (vt)	[kɔ̃prɑ̃dr]
to wait (vt)	attendre (vt)	[atɑ̃dr]
to want (wish, desire)	vouloir (vt)	[vulwar]
to work (vi)	travailler (vi)	[travaje]
to write (vt)	écrire (vt)	[ekrir]